Sacr

T0376449

“In the opening pages of Mic… learn the astonishing fact that the name of the Sanskrit script, *devanāgarī*, means ‘city of God.’ An alphabet understood as both divine and human, a sociality of fire. Drawing from his years as a student of yoga and Indian spirituality, Sowder meditates on the revelatory proximity of language, holiness, and embodiment in this elegant volume. He reflects on our most humane impulses as connected beads along a chain and as beauties worthy of contemplation for their own sake, his developing narrative fusing the personal to the mythic, to the transformation of both. ‘The teacher comes singing,’ Sowder writes; we his readers are fortunate to listen.” —**Kimberly Johnson, PhD**, poet; National Endowment for the Arts scholar; professor of classics, Brigham Young University

“*Sacred Letters* is a tantric text, woven of two gorgeous books. First, in clear bell-like tones, Michael Sowder provides instruction to the Sanskrit language, its sounds and syllabic letters. The second book, vivid as last night’s dream, is a pensées. It strings memories, visions, and reflections on a thread of sound. Follow the thread: a host of teachers—from gnarled old-apple Thoreau to radiant Mā Indirā Devī—lead you by torchlight up the mountain of yoga.” —**Andrew Schelling**, author of *Love and the Turning Seasons: India’s Poetry of Erotic and Spiritual Longing*

“Rather than confining words to their original origins or etymology, this book invites them into a broader, personal context, blending them into a cultural and philosophical framework. It is a rich intersection where philosophy meets life.” —**Semeen Ali**, poetry editor, *Muse India*

“*Sacred Letters* evokes and embodies the living breath of meditation and heart-centered contemplation in this inspired journey through the Sanskrit ‘alphabet’ and its many archetypal permutations. These masterful meditations uplift readers with him into the realm of the ecstatic yet remain solidly anchored in the felt material world, where the personal, historical, mythic and spiritual all meet.” —**Alan Botsford**, author of *Walt Whitman of Cosmic Folklore*

"Sowder presents fifty Sanskrit letters as doorways into profound insights about yoga philosophy, mystic revelations, natural beauty, holy pilgrimages, and a spiritual memoir of awakenings. Each letter reveals a brilliant aspect of divine love, like the many facets of a diamond." —**Robert Sternau**, poetry editor, *Sufi Journal*

"Sowder charts his spiritual awakening, powerfully captured in life's moments when the divine and the everyday intersect. With a poet's eye and a scholar's mind, he rescues these epiphanies from forgetfulness and illuminates them for fellow seekers." —**Sue William Silverman**, author, *How to Survive Death and Other Inconveniences*

sacred letters

Sanskrit, Yoga, and Awakening the Divine

MICHAEL DAVID SOWDER

MONKFISH
BOOK PUBLISHING COMPANY
RHINEBECK, NEW YORK

Sacred Letters: Sanskrit, Yoga, and Awakening the Divine Copyright © 2025 by Michael David Sowder

All rights reserved. No part of this book may be used or reproduced in any manner without the consent of the publisher except for in critical articles or reviews. Contact the publisher for information.

Paperback ISBN 9781958972823
eBook ISBN 9781958972830

Library of Congress Cataloging-in-Publication Data

Names: Sowder, Michael, 1956- author
Title: Sacred letters : sanskrit, yoga, and awakening the divine / Michael David Sowder.
Description: Rhinebeck, New York : Monkfish Book Publishing Company, [2025]
Identifiers: LCCN 2025011030 (print) | LCCN 2025011031 (ebook) | ISBN 9781958972823 paperback | ISBN 9781958972830 ebook
Subjects: LCSH: Sanskrit language--Alphabet | Sanskrit language--Alphabet--Religious aspects | Sanskrit language--Alphabet--Philosophy | Yoga
Classification: LCC PK689 .S69 2025 (print) | LCC PK689 (ebook) | DDC 491/.211--dc23/eng/20250418
LC record available at https://lccn.loc.gov/2025011030
LC ebook record available at https://lccn.loc.gov/2025011031

Book and cover design by Colin Rolfe

Monkfish Book Publishing Company
22 East Market Street, Suite 304
Rhinebeck, New York 12572
(845) 876-4861
monkfishpublishing.com

For Jennifer, Aidan, and Kellen,

For my mother, Kathleen Wall Sowder,

my Sanskrit teachers,
Dr. Ravi Gupta, Dr. Antonia Ruppel, & Niall Mandal

and

my Guru, Mā Indirā Devī

The thousand-syllabled voice in sublimest heaven,
From Her descended in streams the oceans of water,
. . . immortal waters, and the universe assumed life.
—*Rgveda* 1.164.41-42

Contents

Part One: *Gopuram* (Entrance)

Personal Note and Acknowledgments 3
Western Yoga and Cultural Appropriation 10
About the Devanāgarī Script and the Letters of Sanskrit 12

Part Two: The Sacred Letters

First Words			17
अ	*a*	First letter	20
अ	*a*	अग्नि *agni:* Fire, the god of fire	21
अ	*a*	अपरिग्रह *aparigraha:* Non-attachment	22
आ	*ā*	आनन्द् *ānanda:* Bliss	23
इ	*i*	इच्छा *icchā:* Desire	25
ई	*ī*	ईश्वर *īśvara*: Lord of the Universe, master, owner of beautiful, ruler of choices and blessings, the Beloved, the Absolute	27
उ	*u*		29
उ	*u*	उषस् *uṣas:* Goddess of Dawn	30
ऊ	*ū*		31
ऋ	*ṛ*	ऋषि *ṛṣi:* Sage, father	33
ॠ	*ṝ*		35
ऌ	*ḷ*		36
ॡ	*ḹ*		37
ए	*e*	एक *eka:* One	38
ऐ	*ai*		39
ओ	*o*	ॐ *Oṃ:* First movement of creation, cosmic sound	40
औ	*au*		42

क	*k*		44
ख	*kh*		46
ग	*g*	गङ्गा *gaṅgā:* Ganges, sacred river	47
घ	*gh*		49
ङ	*ṅ*		51
च	*c*	चमत्कार *camatkāra:* Astonishment, rapture	52
छ	*ch*	छाया *chāyā:* Shadow	54
ज	*j*	जगत् *jagat:* Universe; ज्योति *jyoti:* Divine light	56
झ	*jh*		58
ञ	ñ		59
ट	*ṭ*	टङ्क *ṭaṅka:* Spade, a hatchet, a stone-cutter's chisel	60
ठ	*ṭh*		62
ड	ḍ		63
ढ	*ḍh*	ढक्कारी *ḍhakkārī:* Name of the Goddess, Tara	64
ण	*ṇ*		66
त	*t*	तत् *tat:* That	68
थ	*th*	थरथराय *tharatharāya:* To grow giddy, to tumble	69
द	*d*	दक्षिणेश्वर *Dakṣiṇeśvara:* City outside Kolkata	70
ध	*dh*	ध्यान *dhyāna:* Meditation	72
न	*n*		74
प	*p*	पुरुष *puruṣa:* First Person, Cosmic Being	76
फ	*ph*	फण *phaṇa*: The expanded hood or neck of a serpent	78
ब	*b*	ब्रह्मन् *brahman*:Expansion, growth, a swelling of the soul, Absolute Divine Reality	80
भ	*bh*	भक्ति *bhakti:* Love, participation, devotion to the Divine	82
म	*m*	मातृका *mātṛkā:* Mother goddess of the alphabet, of all things	84
य	*y*	योग *yoga:* Union	85
र	*r*	रस *rasa:* Essence, the finest part of anything	86
ल	*l*	लीला *līlā:* Play	88
व	*v*	वाच् *vāc:* Sound, voice, word, name of the Goddess	90
श	*ś*	शून्यता śūnyatā: Emptiness, absence, void	92
ष	*ṣ*		94
स	*s*	स्थान *sthāna:* Place of articulation;	95
		संन्यासि *saṃnyāsi:* Ascetic, renunciate	96
ह	*h*	हिम् *him:* Vedic predecessor to *Oṃ*	97

.	ṃ	अनुस्वार *anusvāra*: A symbol / letter / sound marked by a dot above or below the line in Indic scripts for a nasal sound, typically transliterated, "ṃ"	98
:	*ḥ*	विसर्ग *visarga:* A symbol / letter / sound of aspiration at the end of a word, marked by two perpendicular dots ":"	99
अ	*a*	अनाहत *anāhata*: Return to First Letter, Unstruck sound	100

Part Three: *Bhāṣya* (Commentary)

Hinduism, Yoga and Renunciate Life, Bhakti, Tantra 105
Notes on the Meditations 111
Permissions 113
About the Author 115

part one

Gopuram
(Entrance)

Personal Note and Acknowledgments

I cannot describe my own spiritual awakening without also expressing gratitude to my teachers, mentors, and friends. Therefore, I'd like to do both here. My journey on the path of yoga began nearly fifty years ago. I was born into an Irish Catholic family in Cincinnati, Ohio, and when I was nine, my father's company moved us to Birmingham, Alabama. I received eleven years of formal Catholic education, but never wholly felt at home in the Church. In high school in the early nineteen-seventies, I began a process of leaving the Church, having discovered psychedelics and riding a wave of the ebbing tide of the sixties counterculture. Then, in my freshman year of college, I discovered yoga, Indian spirituality, and Sanskrit. It began as I read the conclusion to Henry David Thoreau's *Walden* in my college English reader. "'They pretend,' as I hear, 'that the verses of Kabir have four different senses; illusion, spirit, intellect, and the exoteric doctrine of the Vedas.'" Little did I know that Kabir would one day become my favorite poet, Thoreau would become my first guru, and Sanskrit and Indian spirituality would become central to my life.

My professor, Dr. Theodore Haddin, showed me the way. One day in class, perhaps before or after he played his violin for us, he exclaimed, "Why, I have read *Walden* like it was the only book in the world!" His comment I date as the beginning of my spiritual life. I checked out a copy of *Walden* from the library, and it became my constant companion. I read and reread it—ever astonished—and by the end of my college career had much of it by heart. I took a course from Dr. Haddin in American Transcendentalism and Indian Philosophy and fell ever deeper in love with these traditions. Having recently passed away at age 91, Ted remained one of my closest lifelong friends. Thank you, Ted.

Dr. James Mersmann, my college creative writing and poetry professor, introduced me to Walt Whitman, who became my second literary and spiritual guru and about whom I would eventually write a dissertation at the University of Michigan and my one scholarly book, *Whitman's Ecstatic Union*. Even though Whitman slyly admonished himself in his journal, to never cite any other author, one of the authors he relied on heavily was Ralph Waldo Emerson. Emerson had studied Sanskrit texts like the *Bhagavad Gītā*, and he and Thoreau introduced Indian philosophy to America. Thoreau was the first American to call himself a yogi. I bought a copy of the *Gītā*, in Christopher Isherwood and Swamī Prabhavānanda's translation, and hoped to one day read it in the original. Jim Mersmann also introduced me to the Indian poet Kabir through Robert Bly's sublime translations. Jim remains one of my dearest mentors and friends. Thank you, Jim. How could I have been so lucky to find these two professors in Birmingham, Alabama, in the late 1970s?

In the spiritual books I was reading, the writers often talked about meditation, but how did one actually do it? I was about the find out. One day, in the English department hallway I saw a poster for a "Free Meditation Class." I bravely showed up on Thursday night. The class was taught by Neil Pharr (Sanskrit name, Nīlakeśava) a bald, bearded man with the most intense, loving blue eyes I'd ever gazed into. Two class members I happened to know from my Catholic high school, Ray Thornton (Rajendra) and Jann Alfano (Jiva Devī). They became my closest friends and fellow yogis. Through Neil's teaching and mentorship, we plunged into the philosophy and practice of yoga, meditation, tantra, and the chanting of mantras. Over the years, we were graced in achieving sublime heights of spiritual ecstasy.

Neil arranged for us to be initiated into the tantric tradition he taught in, *Ānanda Mārga,* by a monk named Dādājī Rudranāth, who was traveling through the Southeast. We received personal mantras and Sanskrit names. In the following years, I would be mentored by another monk, Dādājī Devadatta, who would give me a series of secret tantric meditation lessons. These monks had been sent to North America by our Indian guru, Shrii Shrii Anandamurti, to spread the teachings of yoga. We sponsored social service projects inspired by the motto, "Self-Realization and Service to Humanity." After attending a national retreat, I returned to Birmingham and started the first meditation program in the Alabama penal system. A deep bow to all these friends and teachers.

These years were exciting years for me. I was practicing and teaching yoga and meditation when such things were nearly unheard of in the

American South. And as I dove deeper into these traditions, I discovered something else. In the works of Thomas Merton and Evelyn Underhill, I learned that the West has its own contemplative tradition, which no one had told me about in eleven years of daily Catholic education! I read accounts of spiritual experiences by Thomas Merton, St. Teresa of Avila, St. John of the Cross, and Meister Eckhart, which closely mirrored those of Indian yogis like Yogānanda, Rāmākrishna, and in the *Upaniṣads*. So many late Friday nights I sat alone in the university library, poring over these mystical and poetic texts. I wanted to read all the books in the library!

Before long I began to feel that I was being called to become a yogic monk, to serve humanity by sharing the spiritual gifts I'd received. Such a move would require relinquishing my love of poetry and writing and eventually leaving my family, being sent to another country, and never seeing them again. So, after college, I lived for a year in our ashram on Sullivan's Island, Charleston, South Carolina, a stop-over on my way to India to become a monk. I studied Sanskrit sitting on our cedar deck, as waves crashed upon the beach beyond the dunes behind our house.

Toward the end of my year there, however, I came upon something that radically changed my plans. I learned about the guru's teachings on using revolutionary violence to bring about social change. I was shocked. I had been steeped in the ideals of Thoreau, Gandhi, Martin Luther King, Jr., and Mother Teresa. I knew I couldn't take lifetime vows within such an order, even though I had dedicated five years of my life to its tradition and its guru. I was thrown into a spiritual crisis.

I left *Ānanda Mārga*, got married, and went to law school—hoping to serve the world in another way. I read the works of J. Krishnamurti, made my way to Zen Buddhism, became a Buddhist, and more or less an atheist. Then, in 1989, I was graced with a spontaneous enlightenment experience. I came to see that the contemplative traditions of the world, through the imperfect medium of language, point toward a single Metaphysical Reality, whose nature is infinite bliss, infinite love and infinite compassion, but which is beyond name, concept, form and time, but not beyond experience.

Perhaps unsurprisingly, I was unhappy as a lawyer. I went through a difficult divorce and began therapy with a great therapist, Robin Kennedy in Atlanta. Through her mentorship and guidance, I left law, obtained my

MFA in poetry writing, studying with the poet David Bottoms, and then a PhD in literature at the University of Michigan. At Michigan, I met my partner, Jennifer Sinor, and we began our life together as writers, teachers, and aspirants on the spiritual path. Eventually, I became an English professor and poet at Utah State University. Many thanks to Robin and the other amazing therapists I have seen.

During the years of practicing as a Buddhist, living in Logan, Utah, I became a leader of a local Buddhist sangha, but I was missing the sweetness of bhakti—the love and devotion so central to the yogic path, central as well as to the path of the Sufi poets and the Christian mystics. Then, in the year 2,000 two things began to happen. First, I entered a painful dark night of the soul. Whenever I sat for meditation, I was plunged into sorrow. A dark, raw, painful feeling filled my heart and body. I didn't know its source, but the sorrow felt old, even ancient. For ten years, the only thing that kept me returning to my meditation was that afterwards I somehow felt a little lighter.

The second thing that happened was that as I went deeper into this dark, raw, painful night of prayer, I began to feel something else, the sense of a presence with me. I didn't know who or what it was but it seemed to hold me as I moved through this grief work, held me like a mother rocking a hurt child. It was unmistakably female. I searched the world's religions for who it might be. Was it Mary, Sophia, Kuan Yin, Tara, Durga, Parvati, Lakshmi, Sarasvati? I filled my altar and walls with statues and pictures of them all. But none felt exactly right. So, I just surrendered into its mysterious presence. It helped me move through the grief, hour by hour, day by day, slow year by slow year.

Over time, I noticed that when I entered the pain fully, without resistance, it seemed less like pain and more just like a kind of energy or electricity. After eight or nine years, I began to notice that I was feeling times of peace and bliss again. My meditations started slowly oscillating between pain and bliss, pain and joy, pain and gladness. One morning, as I moved between these two opposites, I realized that the two were the same thing! The pain and bliss two manifestations of a single fierce, fiery energy. And then, my second awakening broke over me like a sunrise.

I saw on my bookshelf a book I had read in the seventies, *Pilgrims of the Stars*, and thought I might read it again. It was a dual autobiography written by two Indian gurus, Dilip Kumār Roy and his disciple, Indirā

Devī. I had read the book decades before but I was then on my way to becoming a monk in a different tradition.

I was inspired by Dilip Kumār Roy's part of the book. And then, on the morning on October 11, 2009, sitting on our sofa, I turned a page and began reading Indirā Devī's words. As I read, I felt I could hear her voice. I *recognized* her voice! I thought, "O, my God, I know who this is. This is the presence who has been with me, holding me, helping me all these years."

Her words came across like those of a mother to her lost child. Word by word, sentence by sentence, something started awakening inside me, a wave of indescribable joy flooded my body. I could feel her within me. This was the person who carried me. This was my teacher. My guru. It felt as though I had been looking for her for my entire life, for thousands of lifetimes, and now had found her. Or, that I had been with her for thousands of lifetimes and now had found her again.

Holding the book in my hands, as happened twenty years before, my consciousness just opened out. I felt my awareness, the love of my heart flow out, saturating all things. This bright, blissful, essence or presence, the Ground of Being, suffused all things. I *was* that Presence, that guru, as was everyone and everything. In India it is said, "God, Guru, and Self and one and the same thing." This Presence was God. It was the guru. It was my Self. For three months, I walked around with my feet barely touching the ground. I lived in a state of indescribable ecstasy. I could not work. My rational, logical brain barely functioned.

Luckily, I was on a sabbatical from teaching, but I was unable to write or do research. What I could do was fold laundry. Make dinner. Do dishes. I could stagger down the glittering aisles of grocery stores blissed-out, teary-eyed, brushing shoulders with angels and bodhisattvas who weeks before had been ordinary shoppers with children. For three months, that's what I did. I took care of my family, doing laundry, walking around in a paradise of everyday life.

Since then, my guru has been with me every minute. Holding and guiding me. There are times of course when I turn away, chasing some worldly desire or running from some worldly fear. But then I come to my senses, and return to the path, and there she is, smiling, waiting with open arms, and I am home.

Over the years, I continued my Sanskrit studies, completed a self-study course and attended a Sanskrit study group led by the scholar, Dr. Ravi Gupta, one of my closest friends at Utah State. Along with my friend, Maria Radloff, I studied for two years with the Pāninian Sanskrit teacher Niall Mandal. Eventually, I made my way to Dr. Antonia Ruppel, author of *The Cambridge Introduction to Sanskrit*, whom I consider my Sanskrit guru. She kindly read and corrected all of the Sanskrit in this book. Scholar Ben Williams also read the manuscript and corrected Sanskrit errors. Any remaining errors are mine. My deepest thanks to these mentors, teachers, and friends.

I also want to express my gratitude to friends and fellow travelers on the yogic path. To my first yoga friends, Raphael Thornton (now, Yogeśvara), Jann Alfano Gentle (Jiva Devī), Neil Pharr (Nīlakeśava). My friends in yoga today include Ravi and Amrita Gupta, Antra Sinha-Waters, Emily Perry, Maribeth Evensen-Hengge, Jake Grossman, Chantel Gerfen, Linda Bradak, Josh Fairbanks, Chandi Hammel, Cami Pack, Dan Judd, Claudia Blyth, Alex Baldwin, and Phebe Jensen. Thanks to each and all of you for your support on this journey.

My poetry mentors, in addition to Ted and Jim, mentioned above, include the late David Bottoms, who chaired by MFA thesis, the late James McIntosh, who chaired my dissertation at Michigan, the wonderful poet and Christian mystic Mike Carson, who hired me for my first teaching job, and the late Ford Swetnam, who hired me for my first job as a poet. Deep gratitude goes to my partner Jennifer Sinor and my dear poetry friends Andrew Sofer, Chris Cokinos, and Ben Gusnberg, who have read and commented on essentially every essay and poem I have written, and who have offered abiding support over the years. Jennifer, Andrew, Chris, and Ben read the manuscript of this book and offered priceless advice and suggestions for shaping and revision. A deep bow goes to the members of "Splinters," my writers' group, including Chris and Ben, Jennifer, Charles Waugh, Kathe Lison, and Amber Caron, who have offered sensitive and encouraging readings and sage counsel over many years.

I offer my deep and undying gratitude to my guru, Indirā Devī, who brought me out of darkness and into the light, and continues to do so on a regular basis, and to her guru, Śri Dilip Kumār Roy ("Dādājī"), and to their devotees, my guru brothers and sisters, Sondra and (the late) Tapas Sen, Rajkumar Mantravadi, Priya Chopra, Vinaya Kshirsagar, Karishmā and Udo Knipper, Bhāratī, Manju, Premal and Sādhika Malhotra, and the late Shankarji, all of whom welcomed me into our guru's beloved family.

And finally, my deepest gratitude goes to my partner and fellow pilgrim on the spiritual path, the author and yoga teacher, Jennifer Sinor, who has been my support and a spiritual teacher for me for many years, and to our children Aidan Sowder-Sinor and Kellen Sowder-Sinor—these three, my personal avatars and incarnations in this marvelous, beautiful life.

Western Yoga and Cultural Appropriation

As a non-Indian practitioner and teacher of yoga, I am mindful of contemporary concerns about cultural appropriation. Indian seekers discovered and created the practices of yoga around the beginning of the first millennium BCE. Yoga evolved over the centuries, incorporating elements of other traditions along the way, including Buddhist philosophies and practices, tantra, bhakti, hatha, etc. Today, as ever, gurus and teachers in India work to share yoga's wisdom with the world, because they know it will redeem and heal us.

In his address to the United Nations, in seeking the creation of International Yoga Day, Prime Minister of India Narendra Modi said:

> Yoga is an invaluable gift of India's ancient tradition. It embodies unity of mind and body; thought and action; restraint and fulfillment; harmony between man and nature; a holistic approach to health and well-being.... By changing our lifestyle and creating consciousness, it can help us deal with climate change. Let us work towards adopting an International Yoga Day.

This generosity of spirit we in the West must meet with reverence and gratitude.

In the broader tantric traditions, from which I have received my own practice, devotees are welcomed as members of one family—or *kula*. An ancient text reads: *bhaktir hy aṣṭavidhā hy eṣā yasmin mlecche 'pi vartate | sa viprendro muniḥ śrīmān sa yatiḥ sa ca paṇḍitaḥ.* "Whoever practices this eight-fold devotion, even a foreigner, becomes just like a brāhmin, a sage, an ascetic, a scholar." *Śivadharma* 1.22

The West's commercialization, commodification, and sexualization of yoga, which has proliferated alongside a pervasive ignorance about yoga's ancient roots, exploits this generosity. Yoga risks being reduced to an exercise regimen to help us achieve a commercially-desirable body, when yoga traditionally has been a spiritual way of life dedicated to self-transformation, and blossoming into compassion and *seva*, service to all beings.

Yoga changed my life, as it has millions of others around the world. Let us bow in gratitude for this great gift that India has given the world. Let our practice and teaching be filled with reverence and love for the teachers who have gone before us and the priceless teachings and practices they have left on the path for us.

About the Devanāgarī Script and the Letters of Sanskrit

For more than two thousand years, Sanskrit was as an oral language, one of the earliest offspring of the Indo-European language family, considered sacred by the ancient Vedic peoples of northern India. Its survival was ensured by Vedic priests using complex, precise methods of memorization for the transmission of scripture as well as grammatical works, such as that of the foremost Sanskrit linguist Pānini (ca. fifth century BCE). After many centuries of oral transmission, Sanskrit began to be written down in the first centuries BCE, originally in a script called *Brāhmī*. By the middle of the first millennium CE, the *devanāgarī* script had emerged from *Brāhmī*, and became the script commonly used for writing Sanskrit. *Deva* means "god" or "gods." *Nāgarī* means "of the city." Thus, the name of the script can be translated as can be translated as "the City of God" or "the Script of the City of God."

Technically, *devanāgarī* is not an alphabet but an abugida, a system of syllables written with consonants that contain an inherent vowel sound and markers for varying the vowel sound. The transliteration of *devanāgarī* into Roman script was regularized by the nearly universal adoption of the "International Alphabet of Sanskrit Transliteration." This Romanized alphabet written with diacritical marks effectively transliterates the *devanāgarī* script and reproduces the sounds of Sanskrit.

Different Sanskritists count the letters of the alphabet differently. This book follows the count of my teacher, Sanskrit scholar Dr. Antonia Ruppel, in her *Cambridge Introduction to Sanskrit* (pp. 11-13): 47 letters and two special sounds, *visarga* and *anusvara,* and I, like some, include the sacred syllable, *Oṃ*.

Table 1: *The* devanāgarī *characters*

अ a as in *but*	आ ā as in *father*	इ i as in *bee*, but shorter	ई ī long vowel as in *bee*	उ u as in *put*	ऊ ū as in *fool*	VOWELS
ऋ ṛ short vocalic *r*, as in *father* (US pronunciation)	ॠ ṝ like *ṛ*, but longer	ऌ ḷ short vocalic *l*, as in *table*	(ॡ ḹ*) like *ḷ*, but longer			
ए e long vowel, similar to the first e in *where*	ऐ ai as in *my*	ओ o long vowel, as in *more*	औ au as in loud			

kinds of stops:	unvoiced unaspirated	unvoiced aspirated	voiced unaspirated	voiced aspirated	nasal	
velar stops	क ka unaspirated k, as in *ski*	ख kha aspirated k, as in *cut*	ग ga hard g, as in *golf*	घ gha aspirated g, as in *egghead*	ङ ṅa 'velar' n, as in *sing*	CONSONANTS
palatal stops	च ca unaspirated palatal, as in *charm*	छ cha aspirated c, as in *ranch house*	ज ja *as in jam*	झ jha aspirated *j* (rare); as in *sponge holder*	ञ ña like *-n-* before consonants, *-ny-* before vowels	
retroflex stops	ट ṭa retroflex *t*: see note above	ठ ṭha retroflex aspirated *t*	ड ḍa retroflex *d*	ढ ḍha retroflex aspirated *d*	ण ṇa retroflex *n*	
dental stops	त ta unaspirated *t*, as in *still*	थ tha aspirated *t*, as in *hot-headed; not like English -th-*	द da as in *dance*	ध dha aspirated *d*, as in *mad-house*	न na as in *name*	
labial stops	प pa unaspirated *p*, as in *sports*	फ pha aspirated *p*, as in *upheaval*	ब ba as in *but*	भ bha aspirated *b*, as in *clubhouse*	म ma as in *mother*	
semi-vowels	य ya as in *yes*	र ra as in *run*	ल la as in *leave*	व va as in *water*		
sibilants and *h*	श śa palatal *s*: as in *ship*	ष ṣa retroflex *s*: further back in the mouth than *ś*: as in *wash*	स sa dental s as in *sing*	ह ha as in *house*		

* This sound does not actually appear, but is conventionally listed in this place to complete/balance the system. It will not be discussed further in this book.

(Ruppel, 11).

In the tantric tradition in which I was trained, both the sounds and the visual representations of the *devanāgarī* letters are considered sacred. Their mythological origins reveal their sacral heritage. In tantra, the sounds of the letters are said to have arisen from Lord Shiva's drum as he danced the dance of creation, destruction, and time. The letters appear on the petals of the cakras of the human subtle body and are used as *bīja* ("seed") mantras for meditation. The fifty skulls that garland the neck of the fierce goddess Kālī represent the letters of the Sanskrit alphabet.

The alphabet also has a divine mother—*Mātṛkā*. Scholar Judith Törzsök writes that "*Mātṛkā* is a well-known alphabet goddess mentioned in many tantric texts.... Her name is traditionally explained as the matrix or source (yoni), i.e. the source of all mantras, all śāstras, and in general, of everything that is made of words.... Kṣemarāja [ninth-century tantric philosopher] points out...that she is the cause of the universe."

Each of the meditations in this book is inspired by one of the *devanāgarī* letters, or by one or more of the words that appear under that letter in the Sanskrit dictionary.

part two

The Sacred Letters

First Words

संस्कृतम

saṃskṛtam

The name of the language is *saṃskṛtam*.
Perfected, well-made

देववाणी

Devavāṇī

The name of the language is *devavāṇī*.
The language of the gods

देवनागरी

devanāgarī

The name of the script is *devanāgarī.*
The City of God

मातृका

mātṛkā

Mother Goddess of the Alphabet
She, from whom all words, scriptures, worlds, issue forth

On the world's summit, I bring forth the father,
and my home is in the waters.
I extend over all creatures,
and touch even the heaven with my forehead.
—Rgveda, 10.125.7

शब्दकोश

śabdakośa

Dictionary

It arrives in the mail in blue cloth, *A Sanskrit-English Dictionary: Etymologically and Philologically Arranged with Special Reference to Cognate Indo-European Languages.* (1879). Sir Monier Monier-Williams (1819-99). Used. "Near Fine" Condition. $175.

I cradle it, open it like a book of spells. A strange miscellany. Runes on stones. Tools for transcendence. I turn the giant pages.

Let us find the words that will make us well.

The Letters

अ

a

The first letter

Dr. Ravi Gupta, Sanskrit scholar, says, *Pronounce it like the "a" in "astonish."* The sound pours from the larynx unshaped by mouth or tongue. "It's the first human sound," he says, "a cry of love or pain."

"A" calls forth *Viṣnu*, the high god who cups the universe in his hands. It is the first phoneme of the sacred syllable *Oṃ* (a-u-m), the primordial sound of creation. All the letters come from *a*.

Quiet the mind and you can hear it, a place to begin.

अग्नि

agni

Fire, also, the god of fire

At midnight, ten thousand feet above the sea, in a camp shadowed by a cliff, cleft by a stream teeming with cut-throat trout, I break branches for a fire and wait for my friend. Thunder rumbles in the mountains. Vowels of coyotes circle camp like smoke. *Dog-words.* Older than history. I stir the orange coals. Sparks spiral up through golden aspen leaves.

By light of the fire, I read in a book of forest monks who offered sticks at the feet of their teachers.

tamaso mā jyotir gamaya
From darkness lead me to light.

My father taught me to build a fire. *Lay it out like an altar, stick by stick. Always start with the smallest twigs. Then, one match, no paper.* A lover of wilderness, reciter of poems, he could have been a teacher, a poet, but was burned in the corporate furnaces of the meltdown of Birmingham Steel.

For us.

Tonight, I read how Agni carries the smoke of sacrifice to the sky gods. My father heard the call again, of rivers and forests, and went home to the fire green mountains of North Carolina.

—for Chris Cokinos

अपरिग्रह

aparigraha

Non-attachment

Lord Shiva's come back from Mount Kailash! They say he'll be at the party, decked out in leopard furs, animal bones, and fossil shells. He's been in his cave meditating for ten thousand years! Right now, he's down at the river making leaf-boats with his sons. Yes, one of the boys has an elephant head!

> For years, I thought aparigraha meant turning away—from parents, lovers, children, the reds and yellows of autumn, Eves of Saint Agnes, Moonlight Sonatas. Then, one day I saw it as a dance that turns away from "grasping at" to "caring for."

This morning, sunlight lights the willows of Logan Canyon. I'm making leaf-boats with Aidan and Kellen, eight and ten. We set the boats on the water, and as each one bobs downstream, we yell, *Goodbye! Goodbye!*

Soon, these children will be waving from those decks, or other decks like them, and I'll be standing here, waving back.

Here is the secret to holding on.

Let everything go.

आ

ā

Second letter

Long a, pronounced like the *a* in *father*. I come upon the word,

आनन्द

ānanda

Bliss

Fourteenth-century Meister Eckhart announced to his German congregation—light from stained glass coloring their upturned faces—

You must go beyond God to find God.

In that unfathomable ground of emptiness before God, the sages say, something stirred. They called it सच्चिदानन्द, *saccidānanda*. Pure Being. Pure Consciousness. Pure Bliss.

Puritan theologian Jonathan Edwards wrote, *The first attribute of God is Beauty.*

Dante's rose.

I sit in twilight on limestone cliffs under the arch of a juniper laden with jade-blue berries. September stars waking. Starlight stitches the universe together.

I open a book of Pascal. Upon his death, a servant found sewn in his coat sleeve a paper recounting the moment God appeared:

> *Memorial*
> The year of grace 1654, Monday, 23 November, feast of St. Clement,
> pope and martyr,
> and others in the martyrology.
> Vigil of St. Chrysogonus, martyr, and others.
> From about half past ten at night until about half past midnight,
> FIRE.
> GOD of Abraham, GOD of Isaac, GOD of Jacob
> not of the philosophers and of the learned.
> My God and your God.
> Your GOD will be my God.

"Every moment," Eckhart promised, "God gives birth to the Word, Christ gives birth to Himself, inside you."

Kabir carved into a palm leaf: "I laugh when I hear that the fish in the water is thirsty."

The teacher comes singing.

इ

i

Third letter

Pronounced like the *i* in *give.*

इच्छा

icchā

Desire, wish, want

One sun-struck afternoon in Kingstown, Jamaica, 1979, having come from Kolkata on a world tour, Shrii Shrii Anandamurti, sat in a tea room hung with bougainvillea, plumeria, orange, and yellow trumpet flowers. He'd just been released from prison in India, acquitted for the murder of a disciple. Not permitted to enter the US, he stopped in Jamaica for his North American devotees. Orange-robed, turbaned, black-bearded monks ushered me in to see him.

I prostrated, lay my forehead, belly, hands and feet on the floor. He called me over to him. Then, he asked, "What do you want?" He was bald, with big, black-rimmed glasses. He'd been a railroad clerk. Where were the long locks and the flowing beard I'd learned to love in images of gurus? But he was an avatar, an incarnation of Lord Shiva, Lord of Yoga, and now he was offering me a boon.

What do I want?

Flummoxed, I blurted out, "Should I become a monk?"

I was twenty, burning like a flame, drunk on Transcendentalism. I felt I'd been called to leave home and family, burn my possessions, walk in saffron robes imparting the secrets of tantra, scattering seeds of comic consciousness, performing midnight rites in cremation grounds, igniting the spiritual revolution to save the world from its plunge into capitalist apocalypse.

He shrugged, holding out his palms. He wasn't going to tell me what to do. He said: "You must do something great with your life!"

I never became that monk. How could I never see my mother again? Then, I learned about the guru's teachings on revolutionary violence, his statement that "violence is the essence of life." Around me, spirits of Thoreau, Gandhi, King, Teresa hovered.

I left the guru and his tradition, married a beautiful Charlestonian, and threw my heart into the gray Atlantic. Then, I went to law school.

ई

ī

The fourth letter

Long *i*, pronounced like the *e* in *bee*.

ईश्वर

īśvara

Lord of the Universe, master, owner of beautiful, ruler of choices and blessings, the Beloved, the Absolute.

īśvara -praṇidhāna

Surrender to the Divine

In the *Yoga Sūtras* (400 CE) Patāṇjali says: Seek enlightenment through the eight-fold practice of *aṣṭāṇga* yoga—a system of ethics, asceticism, and meditation. One of these practices is *īśvara-praṇidhāna*, which means, "surrender to the Lord."

In another place in the same sūtras, Patāṇjali says: seek enlightenment through the three-fold practice of *kriyā yoga*. One of which is *īśvara-praṇidhāna*.

Then, in another place, Patāṇjali says: seek enlightenment simply through the practice of *īśvara-praṇidhāna*. Not eight-fold or three-fold, but let us say, one-fold, or, *unfolded*.

To practice *īśvara-praṇidhānam*, you stop fighting, rest your feet on the balustrade, breathe in the lilac breeze. Fall into Daoism's *wu-wei*, "doing without doing," into flow, the zone. Luckily, like Thoreau, we were born just in the nick of time. June leaves opening.

Islam, means *surrender to God*. A simple, unfolded practice.

Hasidism, says, all you need is *dvekut*—love—*cleaving to God*.

I unfold my body, lay my belly, chest, forehead on the temple's cold stone floor, release the violet lilac from my hands.

उ

u

Fifth letter

Pronounced like the *u* in *put*.

Second phoneme of the sacred syllable, *Om*.
A name of the deity, *Shiva*, Lord of Yoga.

Meditating through deep time, covered in ash, friend to cobras, tigers, elephants, peacocks, bulls, Shiva is Lord of the Animals, Lord of Yoga, Lord of Destruction. Androgynously he appears as *ardhanārīśvara*, left side female, right side male. When he dances the *tāṇḍava*, wreathed in fire, he calls up the winds of creation and destruction, spinning worlds off his fingers like pinwheels. His right hand beats the drum of time, a second holds the fire. His left hand points to mother earth, a second, lifted, says: *No fear*. He dances on the demon of our ego.

Magician, Trickster, Yogi. Wizard.

In Switzerland, he dances outside CERN, earth's largest particle collider. At the end of time, he'll blow out the universe like a candle and trigger a new Big Bang.

But you don't have to wait for that. Every second the world goes out and is born. Heraclitus said it. Rivers, breath, body, seas, galaxies vanish and are born, vanish and are born. Every moment annihilated, every moment new.

So, here, we stand at the center. Some cry, "catastrophe!" "Despair!" Just lift your foot to the sound of the drum, the one no one hears!

Oṃ namaḥ Śivāya!

Under our feet, particles colliding at the speed of light.

उ

u

उषस्

uṣas

Goddess of Dawn

I was nineteen, standing in the driveway before sunrise, thinking of Emerson's words about the Self. A dark blue winter Southern sky sphered overhead. In a holly on the hill, a mockingbird woke, flinging grace notes, trills, chattering of the bounty of crimson berries, I supposed. Vines, heavy with dew, draped the loblollies of the dark woods.

Then sunlight shot through, and the vines burst into ten thousand prisms. I spun around seeing gold, red, silver, blue, until something—the day, the world, my mind, my heart—broke open.

The mockingbird flew up, singing that we would live forever, all the words written on its wings.

ऊ

ū

Sixth letter

Pronounced like the *u* in *blue*.

ऊ

A name of Shiva, the moon, a cry for compassion, a promise to care for, the sound of sewing, weaving.

I light candles, set a picture of my mother and my guru on a make-shift altar and close my eyes. Outside, monkeys and peacocks crying. When I open my eyes, fir needles have splintered the sunlight. A crescent moon crowns the Red Mountain, Arunāchala. I'm staying in a cottage at the ashram of Rāmana Maharshi, Tiruvannamalai, India.

I open the dictionary and find words under the letter, ū:

ūdha, borne, carried.

ūti, weaving, sewing.

ūdhan, an udder, a cloud.

ūdhanya, milk.

ūrmi, a wave, a pleat. Distress. *Compare: māli*, wreathed or adorned with waves; hence, the ocean.

ūrmika, a finger ring, something shining like a wave. The hum of a bee, sorrow for things lost.

Then, the morning darkens. Clouds catch their hems on the peak. Rain rains. What is borne by all this water? *Memories. Mother.* I can see her sewing by a window, humming her favorite tune, Tchaikovsky's Fifth Symphony, Second Movement. Her needle shining like a finger ring.

When the sky clears, I look for her in the moon, unmoored crescent, sailing through clouds. Somewhere, she is stitching *sūtras*, the scriptures of tomorrow.

Once, in a vision, I saw the universe dissolving and being born.
She was wreathed in lamplight, adorned with adagio waves.

ऋ

ṛ

Seventh letter

Pronounced like the *r* in seer, *father*.

ऋषि

ṛṣi

Poet, father, seer, sage

Think of all those prophets!

Seven seers, *ṛṣis*, heard the vedic hymns of perigee and apogee. Seraphim touched Isaiah's tongue with a burning ember from the altar of God. Into a cloud of fire walked Moses, and he heard the voice, *I am, I am*. Tiresias turned blind, turned female, to read leaves of the prophesy. And no one cared about Cassandra murmuring of Clytemnestra's mariticide? Munching locusts, the Baptist spat out carapaces and lizards' feet, washing new apostles for The End of Times.

Gabriel brought news of a son to Mary, and shepherds gazed up into angelic theophanies, while their sheep tore grass out of the snow.

Nāgārjuna, Sorcerer of Emptiness, stole from serpents the lost revelations of the Buddha! And in Hira cave, Muhammed prayed and fasted, fasted and prayed until Gabriel came and held up a veil with golden letters, commanding Muhammed to *Read!* Joan of Arc heard a quiet voice and began sharpening her father's sword.

In a castle, St. Teresa found the Bridegroom's chamber. And, Milton staged the birth of the One Light. Joseph Smith read gold tablets with magic seer stones, and Whitman set the type for the New American Bible. Half a world away, Ramakrishna tracked God to center of the atom but found His tent pitched in a canyon of the heart.

Forgive them.

They tried to write the music that they heard.

And who will be our seer now, as we spin our planet into flame? Who can hear the music of the turning spheres?

Listen carefully, my friend. The only *ṛṣi* now is you.

ॠ

ṝ

Eighth letter

Pronounced like *r* but longer.

An exclamation of terror.
A name of Bhairava, a terrible form of Shiva.
Also, the Mother of the Gods,
Mother of demons,
a breast.

Why so many terrifying images of God?

Sir Edmond Burke, in 1757, essayed the difference between "the sublime" and "the beautiful." Cataracts and chasms versus daisies and daffodils. The sublime, he said, must always have an element of terror. Storms at sea. Lightning exploding an oak.

What was your face like before you were born? The Buddha asked. At his birth, Aidan's face was a purple screaming emergency. And back beyond that? Only the Mother.

We went to Disneyland, Splash Mountain. Aidan, five years old, wouldn't get in the roller coaster. Why should he have? We'll pay for a thrill when we can see the happy ending.

Terror marks our limit.

ऌ

ḷ

Ninth letter

Pronounced like the *l* in *table.*
ḷ appears only in forms of the root word,

kḷp

To produce

The letter itself stands for a mountain,
the earth,
the Mother of the gods.

Back before the birth of the gods, *mātṛkā*, the Mother, rested. From Her, *śabda*, sound, arose. A humming, issuing forth as *Oṃ*. *Oṃ* gave birth to fifty fractal sounds, then letters, gods, galaxies, planets, plants, animals, humans, the cosmic warp and woof of space and time. Spacetime.

All this unfolding unfolded inside you.

ॡ

ḹ

The tenth letter

Pronounced like *ḷ*, but longer.

Entirely artificial and only appearing in the works of some grammarians and lexicographers.
—Monier-Williams

There is no letter *lī*. Still, we find meanings for the letter, itself:

A name of Shiva. Also, the mother of the wish-fulfilling cow, *kāmadhenu*, who grants all desires and incarnates as terrestrial cows.

I read that all the gods live in *kāmadhenu*. Her legs the scriptures. Her horns the Trinity. Her eyes the sun and moon. Her shoulders hold Fire-God Agni and Wind-God Vāyu.

Kāmadhenu, the wish-fulfilling cow, grants all the desires of all the people, and, yet, she was born of ḹ, which does not exist.

Just like these thoughts. These words come forth from nothing. The emptiness where nothing takes place and everything is born.

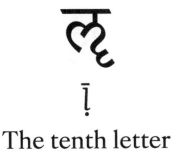

ए

e

Eleventh letter

Pronounced like the *e* in *egg.*

एक

eka

One

ऐ

ai

Twelfth letter

Pronounced like the *y* in *sky*.

The letter is an interjection, a name of Lord Shiva, Auspicious One.

aindra
A name of the Goddess, Durgā.
aindrajāla
Of magic, sorcery—*from indrajāla*, "Indra's net."

In the beginning, Indra, the chief of gods, spread out the cosmos like a great blue net. In each knot, he set a jewel of ten thousand facets. Now, every jewel reflects every other. Each being contains all other beings.

This morning, I'm walking home after rain with my child in my arms. Puddles lie around us like fallen pieces of sky. As we walk, Aidan keeps his gaze on me, and I remember how when I was four I saw my face inside my mother's eyes.

At home we walk along the porch where windows hold our faces in their hands. In his bedroom: carved animals, coins, and crayons, stones and cowrie shells. All our lives, collecting tesserae, setting them back into their places.

—for Aidan

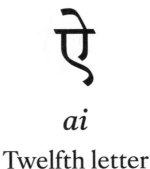

ओ

o

Thirteenth letter

Pronounced like the *o* in *home.*

ॐ

Oṃ

Sacred syllable, first sound of creation

Under the Milky Way, "Star River," which pours snow on Himālayan peaks, people sang hymns around fires in fields, while the lowing of cows filled the night. Mother cows called for their calves, singing *hmmm, hmmm.* And the people sang to the high gods, mantras floating on the steady drone of the lowing of the cows.

> Come, come home, come drink the milk of my body,
> milk of kindness, milk of stars.

The dawn sun shot rays across the land, and the centuries sang on. *Hmmm* became *oṃ*, name of the goddess, *Sarasvatī*, mother.

This morning, mist rises from rills and pools, from heavy dew, where Aidan, seven, and I stir the coals of two fires. Cows graze nearby. We call our camp *Moo City, Cowtown.*

I pour hot cocoa into blue metal cups, speckled with stars, and we listen to the sound of the mothers. I listen for *Devī*, Goddess, calling us home.

—*For Aidan*

औ

au

Fourteenth letter

Pronounced like the *ow* in *cow*.

Today I celebrate words under letter औ.

auṣasa:	Of, belonging to day-break.
Auccḥaiḥśravasaḥ:	Of the chief-of-the-gods, Indra's seven-headed, flying horse.
Aulūka:	A parliament of owls.
Auṣadhi:	An herb that emits fire. Name of the sacred, hallucinogenic soma, lord of plants.
Aupagrastika:	The sun or moon in eclipse.
Auttānapāda:	The pole star.
aupala:	Stony, of stone.
auṣṭra:	Of a camel, abounding in camels.
audhasya:	Milk from an udder.
auṣṭra:	Milk of a camel.
auṣaṇa:	Black pepper.
audbhida:	Fossil salt, rock salt.
aupavastra:	Fasting, food suitable for a fast.
audupika:	A passenger in a boat or raft.
audañcana:	That which is contained in a bucket or pitcher.
audārya:	Being in the womb; generosity, nobility, magnanimity, depth of meaning, stoicism.
aupadeśika:	Living by teaching, got by instruction, as in wealth.

aupacārika: Metaphorical, figurative, secondary.
aupamya: Comparison, simile.
aupaniṣada: Contained or taught in the scriptures, the Upaniṣads.
auṃ: Sacred syllable.

क

k

Fifteenth letter

Pronounced like the *k* in *sky*.

A name of Brahman, Absolute Reality,
of Viṣnu, who holds the universe together, and
sun, soul, time, light, fire, splendor, peacock, joy.

Ka asks the questions: who, where, what? *Kapāla* is a cup, a jar, a dish, the bowl of a beggar, a skull, the cranium. A *kapālin*, follower of a Śaiva sect, who carries a human skull as an ornament and for eating and drinking.

Kaliyuga: the last of four ages of the world. The present age. The dark age. An age of chaos, treachery. The age began at 6:00 a.m., Friday, February 18, 3102, BCE, and will span 1200 years of the gods, or 432,000 human years, at the end of which, the world will be destroyed. And remade.

"Kali" comes from *kala*, the side of a die marked with a single dot. The losing die.

This is the Age of Dice. Millennia ago, people threw dice in the Indus Valley and in Scara Brae, Scotland. Antelope knuckles made fine dice, pips arranged so opposite sides equaled seven. In Ancient Egypt, someone dropped a twenty-sided die in the mud of the Nile. The single oldest known specimen was found in Shahr-e Sukhteh, the Burnt City of Southeast Iran (circa 3,200 BCE) beside the head of a six-foot woman with the first known artificial eye. This eye waited five thousand years to reopen, its iris painted gold, sun rays extending in all directions.

Eckhart said, "The eye with which I see God and the eye with which God sees me are the same eye."

The eye is God's die.

Once, brothers bet a kingdom on a throw, and so began the longest epic in the world. Old Testament *Proverbs* warn, *The lot is cast in the lap, but every decision is the Lord's.* Caesar, resolved to attack the Eternal City, reigned his horse on the bank of the Rubicon and cried, "The die is cast!" Meanwhile, back in Rome, lounging in the Forum, Praetorian guards played dice on a board cut in stone, where two thousand years later, I brush my fingers.

Kula means "family." Wedding rings are gold dice The desk of your first job was full of nothing but dice. With egg and sperm, we roll the dice in the hay. Aidan and Kellen throw metal dice of rainbow colors, their Dungeons and Dragons stories already fated.

Holy Mary Mother of God.

Patāṇjali said that in *kaivalya*: the yogic state of liberation, *the seer abides in its own nature.* Plotinus called it *The flight of the alone to the Alone.* So, *kapālin* ascetics walk away. Win-lose, first-last, rich-poor—all that means nothing to them. Bones are bones. Skulls are drinking cups. Saffron robes flutter like flames. Naked yogis are *digambara, clothed with sky*, covered in ash, stardust.

Avatar Krishna came down to say, *Only love defeats the throw.*

So, here, in Kaliyuga, Friend, cast your lots with care. Holdfast to *ka*: sun, soul, time, light, fire, rainbow, peacock, joy.

ख

kh

Sixteenth letter

Pronounced like "ka," with a puff of air.

The sun, a cave, a portal, the temple of the heart, a wound, a hole made by an arrow, space-ether-sky-air-heaven, *brahma*, the creator, a cipher, *sūrya*—the sun god; in grammar, the *anusvāra*, a humming sound, the tenth astrological mansion, a city, a field, *sukha-duḥkha*, joy & suffering, a fountain, a well, flying things, thus, insects, bees, grasshoppers, planets, wind, deities, arrows.

Khaga: moving in air, thus, any bird.

Khagaṅgā: Sky River.

Once, Valmiki, first poet, saw a hunter kill two mating herons with one arrow. In grief, he cursed the hunter, and his metrical curse became the birth of poetry.

Prākāmya, one of eight yogic powers: *To fly through the air like a bird.*

ग

g

Seventeenth letter

Pronounced like the *g* in *gather*.

I stop at the word,

गङ्गा

gaṅgā

Sacred river of India

What can we give to our children?

We went down into the glacial, gray-green waters of the Ganges at Rishikesh. Above us, the temple town shimmered in one-hundred-three-degree June heat. Pouring down out of the Himālayas, the river ran clean and swift and cold.

Women in colorful saris, mothers with girls, walked into the water, bent down for its blessings, and showed us how.

Mā Gaṅgā, river-goddess, Star River that falls from heaven, pouring through Shiva's hair.

All my life I dreamed of coming here. We bow down, our heads go under.

घ

gh

Eighteenth letter

Pronounced like an English "g" with a puff of air.

gha

At the end of a word, meaning, "killing"

Patāṇjali says that the first principle of yoga ethics, *ahiṃsā* (nonviolence), must be the yogi's *mahāvrata*, "great vow." Vyāsa's commentary says the yogi must practice "non-violence toward all beings, in all ways, at all times."

This evening, I raise a flyswatter as high as I can to smash the spider on the sofa. It's as big as my fist. Lime-green guts hit my face. I wipe them with the back of my hand. Jennifer, Aidan and Kellen are playing upstairs. I'm making dinner in our stone cottage in McLeod Ganj, a Himālayan town above Dharamshala where the Dalai Lama and hundreds of Tibetans live. The Indian government has granted them a home-in-exile here. Vibrant and bright-eyed, for seven decades they have come, fleeing the violence of Chinese occupation. Trekking over the mountains under the cover of winter nights.

Each morning under deodar trees, I walk a mile-long pilgrim's path that circumambulates the Dalai Lama's temple. Half way around, a plaza opens with posters of hundreds of Tibetans who have immolated themselves in protest against the occupation. Inside the temple, I perform one hundred and eight prostrations before the altar. I'm a yogi, rather than a Buddhist, but everyone is welcome.

For a month I've killed at least one spider every day. They're more like small animals than bugs. For a month, I've kept Aidan from seeing a single one. He's terrified of spiders. The cottage owner didn't mention the spiders when we booked the cottage. We might not have come. But here under the shadow of the temple of the planet's Prince of Peace, I perform my ritual killing.

I think of the great vow. But, what did Patāṇjali know about the immune system, whose reason for being is continual killing? A monk says, "We cannot live without harming. This is the tragedy of life. So, we dedicate ourselves to serving."

I wash my face, careful not to get water in my mouth, wipe the flyswatter, clean the spot on the sofa, and call my family down for homemade vegetarian pizza.

ङ

ṅ

Nineteenth letter

Pronounced like the *ng* in *sing*.

Monier-Williams's dictionary says: "No word in use begins with this letter." The letter, nevertheless, has meanings (not attested in literature, only in lexicographers' lists): An object of sense, desire for any object, Lord Shiva (*Bhairava*), the verbal root, *ṅu*, "to sound."

No words begin with this letter, which stands for desire and the objects of desire, and for Shiva, conqueror of desire, for his fierce form, *Bhairava*, destroyer of the objects of desire.

It begins no words but begins the verbal root, *ṅu*, "to sound."

What is the sound of desire? That moan. What is the sound of the end of desire?

Tonight, I am listening to the sound of a fire, which, to the Buddha suggested desire and to yogis the end of desire.

What is the sound of snow falling in fire?

च

c

Twentieth letter

Pronounced like the *ch* in *charm*.

चमत्कार

camatkāra

Astonishment, wonder, rapture

Above me a mountain ash spreads a crown of ten thousand leaves shimmering before a cloudless blue—like pieces of jade in lapiz. Out of the branches a kingfisher flies, crying, *where-where-where*? I'm dangling my feet over the edge of summer.

I too want to be lifted into beauty.

And what is beauty? Theologians and philosophers have cracked their heads over it. Is it a snare, like the garden of Spencer's "Bower of Bliss?" Or is it Plato's "ladder of love"—by which beautiful things have been arranged like rungs on a ladder on which we ascend to God? Plying Lake Geneva, St. Bernard averted his eyes from so much earthly glory. The eighth-century Kashmiri *Vijñāna-bhairava-tantra* says to see the world merely as a magic show. And, Buddha, too, pointed to beauty's ephemerality, its essential emptiness. Nietzsche said God was dead, but before that he said that it is "only as an aesthetic phenomenon that the world and all existence can be justified." In spite of everything, the world is beautiful.

I turned away once, too, on my way to becoming a monk.

But the first attribute of God is Beauty, wrote Jonathan Edwards. And Emerson echoed him: *It is not that the world is painted or adorned. But Beauty is the creator of the universe.*

Poet Issa, after his little daughter died, wrote a haiku for his master:

This dewdrop world is but a dewdrop world—
and yet.

And yet—there was a daughter.

I gaze up into this green June jubilee. Ten thousand green fires bursting into ecstasies of flickering light, ten thousand pennants, ten thousand affirmations that all our problems are made-up.

In my fiftieth year, I learned the word *camatkāra: The creator's own rapture, gazing through our eyes, at the universe it has made.*

—for Kellen

छ

ch

Twenty-first letter

Pronounced like an English *ch* with a puff of air.

छाया

chāyā

Shade, shadow, luster, beauty

Once, the Sun's wife ran away from home, leaving only
her shadow, chāyā, to care for
her children. We are those children.

Remember the October night you pulled up to the Clingman's Dome trailhead sometime after ten o'clock for our backpack in the Smokies? You'd come away from your raging wife (dead now ten years). We packed our packs and headed up toward the high ridges of the Appalachian Trial, hiking in earth's shadow toward Ice Water Springs. Moonlight, starlight, lit our way, lit the rose quartz of the mountains. Subalpine firs stood around like Christmas trees, like wilderness guards, black fathers, grey ferns bowing at their feet.

For seven days, we sweetened our lunches with huckleberries, sitting on shaded cliffs at Charlie's Bunion, Chimney Rock, Spence Field, gazing out onto our favorite views and bathed in ice water falls.

It seemed like a return to childhood, to days free in summer, when we lit out after breakfast into Mount Airy Forest, geared up with pocketknives, binoculars, *Diamond* matches, *Winston* cigarettes stolen from Dad's dresser drawers. We lit leaf fires and wildly stamped them out, stogies dangling from our gangster mouths. In cold creeks, we snagged crawfish, tadpoles, jumping frogs, and garter snakes. And at dusk, we hurried home, slipping under the fence of our Dad's trip-wire anger.

A year older than me, you were the better batter, better pitcher, kid-mechanic with radios, motorcycles, cars. And the girls loved you best. Mom would pull up to Our Lady of Sorrows Catholic School, and I bore the squeals, *There's Joe Sowder! There's Joe Sowder!* We fought, too, like brothers, in that Homeric, Darwinian daylight of boyhood. But then one day, like watching a sun going down, you realize there never really was anything to fight about.

Tonight, on a cliff above Logan Canyon, limestone, aspens, and firs gleam in the moonlight. In half-light, this starlight, I think we see more clearly. Mom and Dad are gone. Aunt Eileen, our family saint, is gone. Our childhood homes, our childhoods. So, I close my eyes and enter the great silence, place of cool shadow, the home we never leave, and where from each other we never part.

—for Joseph Sowder

ज

j

Twenty-second letter

Pronounced like the *j* in *joy*.

जगत्

jagat

Universe

ज्योति

jyoti

Divine Light

Morning light streamed over the high walls of the cirque, shadowed by Kintla Peak, the Livingston Range, where the rills of seven waterfalls fell running toward each other to make a stream, where we pitched our tent. The water tumbled white, danced free over the lip of the cliff, off into vast nothingness.

We bowed down to filled our bottles for morning tea. I was chanting, *jagajjyoti, jagajjyoti, light-of-the-world, light-of-the-world.*

One day I will give you a name, *jyotiprema*. Light-of-divine-love, love-of-divine light, divine-light-of-love. Light of Divine Love.

I bow down in that light.

—for Jennifer

झ

jh
Twenty-third letter

Pronounced like *j*, with a puff of air.

The letter, itself, stands for,
Wind accompanied by rain.

Once, I nestled in a down bag in a bunk bed across from a young woman in a three-sided, tin-roofed, stone shelter, high on a ridge in the Appalachians. Outside, a storm thundered. Wind accompanied by rain. Like me, the young woman was hiking alone. I lit a candle, set it on a stone in the wall, and read Marguerite Porete in its light. I was practicing at being a monk.

Earlier, the young woman and I had leapt about exclaiming, "Look! Look!" gazing through the double arc that a sunset rainbow had thrown over the mountain, as though we were gazing into another world. Now thunder shook the shelter. Flashes of blue and silver light.

In the morning, I woke late, rain dripping. No wind. To white light and a humming of bees. A sound like a small surf over pebbles. My mind was empty, a vessel of listening.

Then, I heard footsteps. Was it the sound of the woman returning, or the sound of the one all our hearts are yearning for?

ञ

ñ

Twenty-fourth letter

Pronounced like the *ny* in *banyan.*

Monier-Williams's dictionary lists the following words beginning with ñ, (none found in existing works—only in lexicographers' lists): a singer, a heretic, a jingling sound, an ox, the planet *Śukra* (Venus).

On his way to Kāśi, holy city, astride a white ox, horns painted blue and gold and hung with bells, the heretic sings of the planet *Śukra.*

Call me Shiva, Call me Hijra,
Call me Lucifer, Circe, Crow,
Call me Ishmael, Hecate, Kālī,
Call me Coyote, Loki, Doe.
I am the return
of all you've cast off.
I carry the coin you covet most.
Will you open the gates of the city for me?
Look!
Śukra, morning star, lights my winding way.

—*for Kellen*

ट

ṭ

Twenty-fifth letter

Pronounced like an English "t," with the tongue curled back, touching the roof of the mouth.

टङ्क

ṭaṅka

A spade, a hatchet, a stone-cutter's chisel, a peak or crag shaped like the edge of a hatchet

In early April, I think of this word as I hang from the side of "Theater of Shadows," a cliff cresting above me like the blade of a hatchet. Snow covers the monolith's north face, so Aidan and I cling to south face granite, warmed by the rising sun. Raining down over us, thousands of tiny icicles glitter—falling free. I wonder if they'll hit the ground as ice or water three hundred feet below. But I've got other things to think about.

With my toes wedged on a ledge, I have two slings tied to my harness, the other ends looped through carabiners hooked to anchors in the rock. Technically, I'm safe. Safe as a baby. I can lean back, and the slings hold me. If I think too much about it, though, fear rushes my body, and I count—one, two, three—steadying my breath. I don't look down. I look at the lichen—yellow, orange, chartreuse, clean and brilliant in the sun and wonder about their strange, lonely life up here.

But mostly I stay focused on my job—which is belaying Aidan, who's seventeen and climbing above me, leading the last pitch to the top. He's out of sight now, having gone up over an overhanging roof, toward the hatchet crest. I feed him rope when I feel his tugs. If he falls, he'll yell, and I'll tighten my grip and brace to be pulled into the rock, as the last bolt he's set catches the rope, and the bolt and my weight arrest his fall.

A raven, croaking, brushes past my shoulder.

High up on the cliff with Aidan out of sight, I feel eerily alone. I start to pray, out loud. There's no one to hear. To the crag gods, to my guru, to Shiva, Lord of Mountains, and Parvati, his mountain goddess, I say, *Keep us safe. Thank you for getting us through those tough spots down below.* And I whisper, *Thank you*, to Aidan, the one I carried in a backpack all over the mountains. What's parenting other than keeping our children alive? Now, he's leading three of the four pitches. *The child is father of the man.*

Then, I hear him yell, *Dad! Off belay!*—which means he's anchored in at the top, at last. *Thank God.* He starts pulling up rope, and when I feel the tug on my figure-eight knot, I yell, *That's me!* I unscrew the carabiners, unhook the slings from the rock, clip them to loops on my harness and yell, *Climbing!* I start to ascend, feeling for holds, chanting, *Aidan has me. If I fall, he'll catch me.* Still, I pray as I go, loving the rock, the bright blue and black carabiners, the icicles and the fear, the light, the ravens, the snow, the clouds and sky, and the unearned gift of a son, who brought me here. All the lines and tools and words we use to keep each other alive.

ठ

ṭh

Twenty-sixth letter

Pronounced like *ṭ* with a puff of air.

Monier-Williams says the letter stands for "a loud noise," "(*ṭhaṭham ṭhaṭham ṭhaṃ ṭhaṭham ṭhaṭham ṭhaḥ*, an imitative sound, as of a golden pitcher rolling down steps.)"

Also: the moon's disk, a cypher, a place frequented by all, the deity Shiva.

But after *ṭhaṭham ṭhaṭham ṭhaṃ ṭhaṭham ṭhaṭham ṭhaḥ*, sound of a golden pitcher rolling down steps, what else is needed for contemplation?

A whole world clamors out of the image—a palace in the sun, women in saris, brahmins talking in alcoves, servants attending guests, workers repairing a viaduct.

The echoes reverberate out of a lost world, a "dead" language. The gold pitcher rolling, ringing, tumbling down into this book of phonemes, into my sunlit study.

I speak the sound out loud.

—for Andrew Sofer

ड

ḍ

Twenty-seventh letter

Pronounced like an English "d," with the tongue curled back, touching the roof of the mouth.

A note of trouble, submarine fire, the deity Shiva. I find words for tumult, calamity, an affray, a riot, a screaming newborn child, an idiot, a lizard, a small owl, a gallinule, turtle, wagtail, a pot-herb, musk rat, a low-caste person (living by singing), a string, a swing, and, then,

ḍākinī: "a female imp attending [the goddess] Kālī (feeding on human flesh)."

Why this note of trouble? A crack in the egg, the pot, the wall, the crease in the picture, the poem, the prayer? Why must there always be this imp, this enabler? Caliban. Igor. Always the one, who pulls you toward the dark door, dark stairs, the whiskey, oxycodone, the razor.

Who is this dark twin, your *doppelganger*? *Ḍākinī.*

Find out now, before it's too late!

ढ

ḍh

Twenty-eighth letter

Pronounced like the English "d," the tongue curled back, touching the roof of the mouth, and with a puff of air.

ढक्कारी

ḍhakkārī

A name of the Goddess Tārā, fierce, terrifying, one of the ten goddesses of wisdom

I repeat her mantra:

oṃ aiṃ strīm oṃ aim hrīṃ phat

More terrifying forms!

Eckhart says Jesus cleansing the temple—overturning tables,

breaking vessels, shouting at sellers to get out—is the tale of Jesus cleansing the soul, canceling the interest on our mortgaging our days away.

Resist, and He'll grow terrifying, lay a lion limb against thee! as Hopkins warned.

We have to enter the temple barefoot, naked.

I die because I do not die! Teresa cried.

Then, when all is settled, swept away, stilled, in that quiet, lark-filled courtyard, hung with damask roses, you will hear Him singing.

ण

ṇ
Twenty-ninth letter

Pronounced like the English "n," but with the tongue curled back, touching the roof of the mouth.

No words attested begin with ṇ. Lexicographers say the letter stands for *knowledge*. The English word for knowledge comes from the Greek, gnosis, from the Proto-Indo-European, gno. But Indian schools of knowledge are called *darśana—ways of seeing*. Philosophy moves not by induction or deduction but by vision.

William James said:

> Although so similar to states of feeling, mystical states... are states of insight...illuminations, revelations, and as a rule they carry with them a curious sense of authority for aftertime.

I had walked the path for thirteen years, and then one morning in the apartment of my girlfriend, Virginia, high on Clocktower Hill, in Rome, Georgia. I was sitting in meditation. It was 10 o'clock. I was thirty-three. I was weeping about my father.

Suddenly, I knew that in spite of the conflict I had had with my father, I still loved him. I realized this, and my body started shaking. I began taking big, giant breaths, heaving, like waves coming over me. I couldn't stop it. I got up. I said to Virginia, *I think I'm having a heart attack.*

I lay down on our bed, and then all of a sudden my consciousness just opened up, streamed out of my body in all directions, infinitely, until it filled, became the universe. All sense of the self I thought I was vanished. I was this infinite ocean of quicksilver light, bliss, like Emerson's "transparent eyeball." "I was nothing. I saw all."

I saw forms, things, beings crystalizing and dissolvin back into this sea of light. It was unspeakable love. I felt love for the most infinitesimal things. It was the quenching of every desire. I knew that seeking was at an end. Virginia, beside me on the bed, said, *What is it like? What is it like?* I said, *It's like the line from Kabir!*

I laugh when I hear that the fish
in the water is thirsty.

There was nothing left to seek, to do, but serve. It lasted twenty minutes. It was outside of time. It was a second. It was Eternity.

त

t

Thirtieth letter

Pronounced like the English "t," with the tongue touching the back of the teeth.

तत्

tat

a demonstrative pronoun, meaning,

that

As a word, it barely holds water. Think of *that*.

For this reason, it stands for God.

Hence, the mantra: *tat tvam asi. Thou art That.*

In Mahāyāna Buddhism, we find the word, *tathātā*: "suchness." "The quality of things as they are, before ideas about them, the exact inimitable quality of this moment as it is."

In Judaism, *Ehyeh asher ehyeh*: I am that I am.

थ

th

Thirty-first letter

Pronounced like *t*, with a puff of air.

थरथराय

tharatharāya

To grow giddy, to tumble

My Dearest Guru,

How long since I grew giddy and tumbled like a child?

This path you lead me down, so serious, full of fasting ascetics, penniless renunciates, hermits, ghosts haunting charnel grounds, scholars poring over dead languages, turning palm-leaves of tiny script.

I get up from my desk with a furrowed brow, a headache, and get some aspirin.

O, Guru, grant me the faith of Al-Ḥallāj (858—March 26, 922, Baghdad), who, before being hanged, grew giddy on God's wine, proclaiming: *Under this robe, there is nothing but God!*

And tumbled.

द

d

Thirty-second letter

Pronounced like the English "d,"
with the tongue touching the back of the teeth.

दक्षिणेश्वर

Dakṣiṇeśvara

A village outside Kolkata where a temple to the goddess Mā Kālī looks over Hoogly River, distributary of the Ganges. Here, the mystic guru Ramakrishna Paramahansa lived for thirty years as priest, intoxicated by bliss, thought mad by some, an Incarnation of God by others.

June 24, 2019. My birthday. My family and I stand on a red brick landing in bright June sun and 103 heat before a statue of Mā Kālī. The black idol of the goddess is adorned with lays of jasmine, hibiscus, and marigolds. She wears a garland of fifty skulls, one for each letter of the alphabet.

Smiling down upon us, in her left hand she wields a bloody cleaver, a lower left hand holds a severed head. Her right hand offers boons. Out of her mouth, she sticks a bloody tongue. Her upper right hand is open in *abhaya mudrā*, which says, *No fear*. I gaze into her playful, child-like eyes.

Ramakrishna was in love with her, saw her as the embodiment of Infinite Formless Divine Consciousness, and also of Pure Materiality. Mother, Protector, Creator, Destroyer. He danced before her, meditated, wept, prayed, crawled, leapt like a monkey before her.

Jennifer, Aidan, and Kellen descend the temple steps, but I am rooted here. Something holds me. I feel I could stand here forever.

Then, later, cross-legged on the black and white tiled floor of Ramakrishna's room, we breathe with eyes closed. Sweat runs rivulets down my back, drips from my chest. In this room, he lived and taught, sang and danced. O, avatar, sadguru, divine fool, I've read your every word in the *Gospel of Sri Ramakrishna*. Now, I've walked into your story. A birthday present from my love.

Out under the bronze sun, Prakash, our guide, leads us into one of twelve Shiva temples lining the bank. Far away stretches the silvery river toward a distant shore. Prakash leads us in a ritual of mantras. We offer milk, water, the trident bilva leaf to the Shiva lingam, phallic, aniconic representation of Infinity.

Prakash takes us down to the river to fill our bottles with water. A woman, hip deep in a green and purple sari, motions to us, takes our bottles and hands them to a boy, who dives like a dolphin and comes up glistening, our bottles filled. We give thanks, Namastes, and rupees. Leaving the temple complex, we stop at a wheeled cart where a turbaned man sells us ice cream drumsticks.

September that year, I travel to Richmond, Virginia, where my mother lies on her death bed at my sister Nancy's house. Nancy has cared for her now for years. I feed my mom vanilla pudding with a spoon, the way she once fed me. She is the one who taught me how to be kind.

On the day I have to leave, I kiss her and say, *Goodbye*. I brush her forehead and touch her lips with water from the Ganges River, from Ramakrishna's temple, at Dakṣiṇeśvara, for her journey home.

—for Nancy Sowder

ध

dh

Thirty-third letter

Pronounced like *d*, with a puff of air.

ध्यान

dhyāna

Meditation

When Dadaji Rudranath, a Tantric monk sent to America by the Indian guru, Shri Shri Anandamuriti, initiated me into *Ānanda Mārga*, the Path of Bliss, we were sitting together cross-legged, face-to-face, on the floor of an upstairs room in an antebellum mansion in Birmingham, Alabama. His orange robes and turban radiated afternoon light streaming in the windows. With eyes closed, he led me in an initiation, gave me my Sanskrit name and secret mantra, a two-word phrase that summed up all the teachings of all the scriptures of the world, with a sound vibration that would make me one with God.

But rather than bathing in yogic bliss, I was preoccupied at the moment with my unworthiness—all the things a college kid might worry about, sins I'd committed, lusts, masturbation. And just as that thought came into my head, Dada said, with eyes still closed, "You should never mis-utilize your energy."

Now—whether the ancient practice of onanism stains one with sin worthy of the flames of hell, as the Catholic priests I grew up with taught (of course, Dada, too, was a celibate), or liberates one via a revolutionary act, free to all—God's gift to rich and poor—as my feminist therapist later would say—the fact that Dada Rudranath could read my mind forever sealed my faith in meditation, mantras, yogic powers, *dhyāna*.

न

n

Thirty-fourth letter

Pronounced like the English *n*.

> Now therefore the description (of Brahman): *Neti neti. 'Not this, not this.' Because there is no other and more appropriate description than this Neti neti. 'Not this. Not this.'*
>
> —*Bṛhadāraṇyakopaniṣad.* 2.3.6.

> *The more we climb, the more language falters, and when we have moved to the top of our ascent, language will turn silent completely, since we will be near to the One which is indescribable.*
>
> —Pseudo-Dionysius

> *To be one with God, there must be in you nothing imagined or imaged forth, so that nothing is covered up in you that is not discovered or cast out.*
>
> —*Meister Eckhart*

In English, words that begin with "n" include: negate, neither, never, nil, nix, no, nor, not.) In *Sanskrit, Neti, neti, neti, neti.*

No no no no no no no no. No no no no no no no no. Not not not not not not not not. Not not not not not not not not. Not that, not that, not that, not that. It's not what you think, it's not what you think. Don't think, don't think, don't think, don't think. It's

not what you think, don't think, don't think. Not that not that not that not that. Not that not that not that not that.

O, Jesus Christ!

Not that, not Christ. Not Yahweh, Buddha, Krishna, Allah, Mary, Kali, Lakśmī, Tara. Not A-vi-lo-ki-teś-va-ra. Not God not God not God not God. Not God not God not God not God. Not dog not dog not dog not dog. Not that not that not that not that. Not cat, not cat, not cat, not cat. Not that not that not that not that.

Thus: no, no not, no not, not no. Not that. No this, no that.

No no. No, this, just this. Just this just this just this just this. This wisp, this wisp, this whispered lisp. Just this just this just this just this. Yes this yes this yes this yes this. This yes this yes this yes yes yes. Yes this this this this this this this. This brink this brink this brick a brack. This lip this cliff this criss—cross—sing.

Just this just this just this just this. This yes this yes this yes this yes. Then light, then light, then light, that breaks. Yes this yes this yes this yes this. This light O light O light O light. No thing no thing no thing no thing. This fire this fire this fire this fire. What's fire? what's fire? what's fire? what's fire? No thing no thing no thing no thing. It is not that it is. It is not what it is. Is what what is? Is that that is? It is is. It is is. It is is. It's it it's it it's it it's it. It's is it's is it's is it's is. It is not that it is. It is not that it is. No thing no thing no thing no thing. It is is it is is it is is it is is. No thing no thing no thing no thing. This this, this this, this whispered lisp. Just this, just this, just this, this I, this I, I am, this I. I am. I am that I am, that I am, that I am. Tat tvam asi tat tvam asi. You are you are you are you are. You are that you are that you are that you are. This beat, this beat, this beat, this beat. This heart this beat, this heart is this. Just this just this just this just this. No thing no thing no thing no thing. I am, you are, we are, it is. No thing no thing no thing no thing. Just this just this just this just this. Just this just this just this just this

—for Ben Gunsberg

प

p

Thirty-fifth letter

Pronounced like the English *p*.

I stop on the word,

पुरुष

puruṣa

Person, Self

In the beginning, *Puruṣa*, First Person, Cosmic Being, dismembered him/her/it-self to fashion the universe. Everything arose out of sacrifice.

The kingfisher swallows the silver leaf with its broken red river, wrote Mary Oliver. We lay our bodies down.

Fantastic!

At dawn, priests chant hymns to the sun, pour grain, ghee, soma into the fire, cut the throat of the youngest lamb. Food for the people, food for the poor!

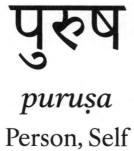

We walk through Kalighat temple, our feet are wet, sticky with blood.

Then, in the middle of the first millennium BCE, the new teachings say:

Carry the pan of fire to the cave of the heart. Find the river, sacred fire. Cut the throat of the lamb of self under the starlit sky.

फ

ph

Thirty-sixth letter

Pronounced like the English *p*, with a puff of air.

फण

phaṇa

“the expanded hood or neck of a serpent”

फणि

phani

one with a *phaṇa*, hence, a serpent, a cobra, also called, a *nāga*

Scriptures say the cobra's *phaṇa* shelters jewels. In the underworld of *nāgaloka*, *nāgas* guard treasures. Their king, a cobra, garlands the neck of Shiva.

Buddha entrusted his secret teachings to *nāgas*, who gave them to Nāgārjuna, a thousand years later.

Once, I sat with a charmer in an orange turban and robes beside a thatched hut. His flute raised cobras from baskets. He showed me how to stroke their *phaṇas* with my fingers.

I have loved snakes and I have killed them.

Above the Himālayan town of Dharamshala, my family hiked to *Saulī Khad*—Shady River—where Jennifer had *darśan* (sight) of a serpent, thick as her thigh, moving through the brush. We did not tell the children.

Now, in a cold dawn, Logan, Utah, I sit before our family altar, incense, candles wreathing statues of Shiva, Durgā, Gaṇeśa, a photo of my guru. The house is cold, and I lift the cowl of my green woolen poncho over my head and think of all the treasures I'm entrusted to care for this side of death, this side of love.

ब

b

Thirty-seventh letter

Pronounced like an English *b*

ब्रह्मन्

brahman

Expansion, growth, a swelling of the soul, Absolute, Divine Reality

Before the sacred fire, priests sang hymns, mantras, posed riddles of creation. The answer to the riddle was called the *brahman*, the mystery, the link that held the worlds together.

Today, the sun rises, and a yellow-headed blackbird chants above our canoe. Its riddles sweet, beyond my ken. You lie back against my body and I read you sacred words. The *Upaniṣads* say Brahman is Infinite Self-Existent Blissful Consciousness, from which all things emerge. Plotinus called it the One. Eckhart, the Ground—God beyond "God."

The *Upaniṣads* say, Brahman and ātman, your indwelling spirit, are One, that the Divine is closer than the breath, the jugular, closer to you than you are to yourself. Why? Because *that* is real and the you you think you are is a bric-a-brac self. Feel the simple sense of presence. That's it!

brahma ātmā asti

Brahman and your Self are one.

A man and a woman and a blackbird are one.

—for Jennifer

भ

bh

Thirty-eighth letter

Pronounced like an English b with a puff of air.

भक्ति

bhakti

Love, participation, devotion to the Divine

Krishna says that in this dark age, *bhakti*, the yoga of love, is the easiest path.

He's right, you know, so long as you don't mind surrendering family and friends, home and possessions, body and soul into the fire.

Jesus crucified showed us the way.

The story of Job is everyone's story. Everything is taken. Meaning, everything is given.

In the fire, you become nothing. Then you become the fire. Then you become becoming.

I know. My guru took me by the hand right into the blaze.

—for Ravi Gupta

म

m

The thirty-ninth letter

pronounced like the English *m*.

The letter names *Devī*, Goddess, Mother.

मातृका

mātṛkā

The alphabet, the mother,
out of whom all sounds, words, scriptures, universes come.
Also, time, moon, magic, death, water.
There is nothing outside the mother.

य

y
Fortieth letter

Pronounced like the English *y*.

योग

yoga
Union

We stand before the Tetons. You hold our son inside. Tall marsh grasses sway in a sunny October breeze. We say vows before a justice of the peace who wears a cowboy hat and a bolo tie. I am crying more than you.

I think, *I will not become a monk in this lifetime.*

That night, we walk past boiling pools of blue, green, aquamarine. Elk bugling. Coyotes howling at our honeymoon.

Your child—say the *Upaniṣads*—is your *atman*, your very self. A man and a woman are one. A man, a woman, a child, and a moon are one.

Kellen, our second, waits in the stars.

र

r

Forty-first letter

pronounced like the English *r*.

रस

rasa

Essence, the finest part of anything, the sap or juice of plants; melted butter, milk, sugar-cane syrup; any mixture, elixir, potion, distillate, quintessence, tincture, perfume; a constituent fluid or essential juice of the body, serum, semen; mercury, quicksilver; essential flavors of foods, of which there are six: sweet, sour, salty, pungent, bitter, astringent; the sentiments of a literary work, of which there are eight (or ten): love, heroism, anger, mirth, disgust, terror, pity, wonder, tranquility, and parental love; religious feelings, *bhakti* (devotion), of which there are five: *śānti* (tranquil awe), *dāsya* (the feeling of a loving servant toward their master), *sākha* (a feeling of friendship); *vātsalya* (the feeling of love of a parent for a child, or child for a parent), *mādhurya* (a feeling of romantic, conjugal love); name of the sacred syllable, *Om*.

One afternoon in my mother's home, three years before she died, I was scrambling eggs, sizzling garlic and green peppers, shredding smoked gouda. I turned toward the fridge and saw on the wall little shelves of tiny bottles—extracts of Vanilla, Almond, Rose, Lavender, Zest of Lemon, Zest of Orange, with worn and stained labels. The same bottles she'd had when I was a child.

What do I know of heaven?

A June afternoon, I was sitting at the kitchen table, legs dangling, as she rolled out dough for lemon pies, my favorite, her hands covered in flour, sweet smells filling the kitchen. She always made two, one for the neighbors, which I could never understand. She was talking quietly, maybe about the cardinals or gladiolas or kindergarten. Outside the big window, honeybees, hummingbirds spun above Dad's garden, the little paradise where I stole peas and tomatoes and peppermint leaves. Beyond that, Mount Airy Forest.

Can I taste? I asked. *It's too bitter*, she said. *But you can smell.* She brought all the bottles over and set them before me. I unscrewed each cap and breathed: vanilla, almond, lemon, orange, rose.

These same bottles.

Rasa of summer, rasa of long afternoons with my mother, of sunlight and June breezes, quiet words and cardinal songs, a yard and a garden.

Rasa of farewell, of irreplaceable gone days in a kitchen, my mom baking my favorite lemon meringue pies.

ल

l

Forty-second letter

Pronounced like the English *l* in *let.*

लीला

līlā

Play

Let's define it as something done for its own sake, its own joy.

All art affirms this or should. We don't listen to Tchaikovsky's Fifth Symphony in order to do something else.

So, on days when I was home and the house was still, in those vast hours of childhood, we built Lego towers to the ceiling, your nimble hands fitting the pieces together, delight in your clear blue eyes, imagination leaping forth like winged Athena.

I made you grilled cheese and tomato soup, and sweet pickles swam like dolphins across your plate—this, before you went away to desks in rows and columns, bell times, and unkind kids.

Later, you made a hundred stop-action films that no one ever saw, designed origami bees, a hundred with a hive you hung from ash branch fitted in a pot for a tree. It won first place, but that's not why.

So many nights, I sat on your floor and sang our family lyrics to Brahms's lullaby, stars aglow on your ceiling, as you flew away to dreams you'd shape the next day with your hands.

Now, I read in an ancient book that the universe was created in *līlā*, revelry, play. Ask what it means, and you miss the point.

There is no point. Just origami bees on an ash branch tree and stop-action films no one has ever seen.

–for Kellen

व

v
Forty-third letter

Pronounced like the English *v* (*or w*).

vāc
Sound, voice, word, name of the Goddess

We dip our paddles in the starry Huron, our canoe gliding silently through the woods, between fields, around bends. Ripples catch moonlight where rocks break the water, murmuring soft as deer hoofs in grass. When the river widens, we lay down our paddles, and you lean back in my arms, listening to a whippoorwill's song.

Ancient seers heard the song of the river goddess Sarasvati:

From Her,
the thousand-syllabled voice in sublimest heaven,
from Her descended in streams the oceans of water.
from her whence immortal waters flow.
from her the universe assumes life.

I look down on your face. Your green eyes catch moonlight. Eckhart says, God gives birth to the Word inside us. What is that Word? This Word? This world?

You are not yet thirty. I recite poems as I angle the oar for a rudder. Poetry began with rowing, the Greeks said. Around a bend, a great blue heron opens enormous wings, lifts its great blue body impossibly off the water.

And I hear the sound of a word, a name. I cannot speak it yet.

Twenty years from now, memory will return, and I will call you:

jyotiprema, jyotiprema,
lightofdivinelove, lightofdivinelove, lightofdivinelove.

—for Jennifer

श

ś

Forty-fourth letter

Pronounced like the English *sh*, in *she*.

शून्यता

śūnyatā

Emptiness, absence, void

Now, my mother, father, and aunt Eileen are gone. But gone where?

Every family creates a miniature culture: rituals, stories, jokes, vacations, meals. On Christmas Eve, each of us opened a present with nutmeg eggnog, and being good Irish Catholics, rather than milk and cookies, we left a shot of whiskey for old Saint Nick. I remember Dad's BBQ chicken, salads of sliced tomatoes, cucumbers, onions in vinegar, a whole ham in the fridge for sandwiches. Mom's blackberry, cherry, butterscotch, lemon pies. Vacations on Dolphin Island. Dad's and his dad's love of fishing. Eileen, our family saint, arriving from Cincinnati, lighting up the house with stories, gifts, and laughter. We'd read letters from Uncle Joe, whom I never met, who survived war in the jungles of the South Pacific to come home and be killed in a car accident.

So, what remains? Cultures vanish like the rainbow of a lawn sprinkler when the water's turned off, or purple leaves falling from a sweet gum tree.

What is that emptiness into which everything disappears? Eckhart said:

> When I yet stood in my first cause, I had no God and was my own cause: then I wanted nothing and desired nothing, for I was bare being and the knower of myself in the enjoyment of truth.... But when I...received my created being, then I had a God. For before there were creatures, God was not "God." He was That which He was.

The Heart Sūtra says, *Form is none other than emptiness. Emptiness none other than form. Form is exactly emptiness. Emptiness exactly form.*

One day, you see the universe dissolve like a snow flake on your gloved hand. Then reappear.

There and not there, here and not here. This is another name for God.

Nothing gone, nothing lost.

Look in the palm of your hand.

ष

ṣ
Forty-fifth letter

Pronounced like the English *sh*, but further back in the mouth, as in *wish*.

The best, the excellent; the wise, the learned; loss, destruction; the end, the term; the rest, remainder; happiness, emancipation; heaven, paradise; sleep; a learned man, a teacher; a nipple.

Every scholar knows that every word in Sanskrit means itself, its opposite, the name of god, and a position in sexual intercourse.

Hallelujiah!

स

s

Forty-sixth letter

Pronounced like an English *s*.

स्थान

sthāna

Place of articulation

You pronounce the twenty-five consonants at five places in groups of five: throat, palate, roof, teeth, lips.

I was sitting in meditation in a lamp dark chamber off the main temple of Rāmana Maharshi's ashram, Tiruvannamalai, India. The walls echoed voices of priests chanting hymns from the Vedas. Outside, on the high roofs, peacocks cried out, joining in.

I chanted too in this crazy, sacred cacophony.

Om namaḥ Śivāya!

O, dichosa ventura!

I think I am learning to speak.

In my pilgrim's bungalow, I open the dictionary and come upon the word,

संन्यासि

saṃnyāsi

Monk, ascetic, renunciate

When you take vows, you burn everything—books, money, clothes, photos.

Kabir says he's burned down his house. He holds the torch in his hand. If you want to follow him, he'll burn down your house, too!

Say, goodbye, to mother, father, brother, sister, wife, said Jesus, if you want to follow him.

I never became that monk. I found another way. A different kind of sacrifice. Partner, children, work, friends—avatars, your incarnations all.

ह

h

Forty-seventh letter

Pronounced like the English *h*.

him

Before the sound of *Om*, the sacred sound was *him*, onomatopoetic for a cow lowing for her calves, onomatopoetic for the first sound of creation, onomatopoetic for vāc, voice out of the Void, Mother, Goddess.

Then, pure sound split into letters, then all the forms of the universe.

Now we chant, and the sounds carry us back.

Deep calls unto deep.

•

ṃ

अनुस्वार

anusvāra

A symbol / letter / sound marked by a dot above or below the line
in Indic scripts for a nasal sound,
typically transliterated, ṃ.

A humming. A drumming.
My mother was sewing, humming by a window.
A sound of bees.
Wind accompanied by rain.
A surf falling over pebbles.

:

ḥ

विसर्ग

visarga

A letter / symbol / sound, called *visarga*,
a distinct aspiration at the end of words,
marked by two perpendicular dots (:).

The letter / symbol / sound meaning: Sending forth, emission, creation; shedding, pouring, casting; a gift; abandonment, relinquishment; voiding, evacuation; the southern course of the sun; the penis; destruction of the world; final beatitude, light, splendor.

Exhalation triggers the vagus, acetylcholine is released, a neurotransmitter. Blood vessels dilate, the heart rate slows.

We sigh in rest.
We sigh at death.
God sighs life into our dust.

अ

a

Return to first letter

अनाहत

anāhata

Unstruck sound. First name of the heart. *There is a place in the soul, Eckhart said, that has never been wounded.*

One night I sat on the sofa of our den, a warm summer breeze stirring the curtains. In the light of a lamp, my mother was ironing, wearing her dark red plaid frock. No one else home. I must have been four or five. The smell of steam rising in puffs filled the air. She was talking, words as gentle as her movements, the quiet *whish* of water becoming air.

This is what I know about love.

Close your eyes in the temple of Indirā. Forehead, belly, feet on the cold stone floor. The inner sanctuary—*garbhagṛha*—the "womb-home."

Stone walls echo with songs from another life.

Mrtyor mā amrtam gamaya.
From death lead me to Immortality.

Let go the lotus in your hands. Hear the sound from before the world began, more ancient than history. In the City of God, a voice from home: mother, father, lover, children. Humming, humming. At the threshold between fire and dark, dream and day.

Caring for, caring for, caring for. Lay it down in the cave of the heart.

part three

Bhāṣya

(Commentary)

Hinduism, Yoga and Renunciate Life, Bhakti, Tantra

This book arises out of a what may be called a non-dualistic, bhakti-tantric tradition of yoga. While most Westerners have encountered the practice of modern postural yoga, not all are as familiar with bhakti, a yogic tradition of devotion, and tantra, an esoteric tradition that contributed significantly to the development of modern yoga. A brief description of these complex and overlapping traditions may be helpful for readers less versed in their particulars.

Hinduism

Tantra, bhakti, and yoga all developed in India within the larger religious landscape of "Hinduism," and each shares features with that over-arching tradition. Hinduism is sometimes described by scholars as an expression of "polymorphic monotheism." There is one God or Ultimate Reality, called Brahman, an Infinite, Divine Consciousness that pervades and transcends the universe. This Divine Consciousness takes the form of numerous gods and goddesses so as to make possible human devotion and personal relationship with Deity. All the gods and goddesses of India are mediums, vessels, vehicles, portals. A user-friendly religion, Hinduism allows each devotee to choose their own *iṣṭadevattā,* their own cherished image for the Divine. This can be a favorite god or goddess, an avatar (incarnation, "one who has come down"), or a river or a mountain, etc. Rāma and Krishna, for example, are avatars or incarnations of the god, Viṣnu, who is himself a form of the formless Brahman.

The term "Hindu," and the name "India" were both coined by ancient Persians to refer to the people living in northwest India along the Indus River. The indigenous name for the country is "Bharat," and Bharat will likely be the preferred name in coming years. "Hinduism" has become a kind of umbrella term for the many forms of spirituality practiced in India, exclusive of the minority religions of Islam, Christianity, Judaism, Buddhism, Zoroastrianism, etc. The country is approximately eighty percent Hindu. Many Hindus prefer the name, *Sanātana Dharma*, "the eternal truth or way." A common way to identify a sect or tradition as "Hindu" is to determine whether it looks back to the ancient scriptures of the Vedas as its foundation.

The Vedic scriptures are a collection of sacred hymns composed orally around the beginning of the second millennium BCE in the northwest region of the subcontinent. Devout Hindus consider them to be eternal and to have been revealed to ancient seers, rather than having been "composed." Up until the present time, their hymns have been chanted by Brāhmin priests during fire sacrifices offered to a pantheon of sky gods, sometimes for worldly ends but also as exalted praise for the gods and the beauty of the created world. This Vedic or Brahmanical culture was centered on this fire sacrifice and evolved over time into what we today know as Hinduism.

Over the course of the second and first millennia BCE the corpus of scriptures grew, until the last renditions, a large collection of relatively short texts called the *Upaniṣads* began to appear around the middle of the first millennium BCE (texts of ancient India are notoriously hard to date). Interestingly, the *Upaniṣads* in part taught a radical turn away from the Vedic communal fire sacrifice (even ridiculing it sometimes along with priests and ritual in general). Instead, they turned their attention toward metaphysical and philosophical speculations and advised a personal practice of introspection and meditation. Such practice would lead to enlightenment and liberation from endless cycles of rebirth, suffering, old age, and death.

Some scholars have characterized this emphasis on individual meditation practice as the Vedic fire sacrifice moving inward. Perhaps the central teaching of the *Upaniṣads* is that each individual soul (*ātman*) partakes of the Divine Brahman, the Universal Spirit, Consciousness, or God. A spark of the Divine shines within each of us. The *Upaniṣads* brought novel concepts into the Vedas, including those of karma, reincarnation, and liberation, likely adopted from pre-Buddhist ideas taking shape in northeast India at the time. Even more interesting is that although the *Upaniṣads* constituted a break with traditional Vedic culture, Vedic culture wholly absorbed them, and today, most Hindus would say that the *Upaniṣads* embody the essence of Hinduism.

Whether yoga, bhakti, and tantra are "Hindu" is a complicated question which different people will answer in different ways. Most Hindus will claim yoga and bhakti (if not tantra) as their own, but depending on how one defines yoga and Hinduism, yoga may be older than Hinduism, or may have grown up on the margins of orthodox Hinduism. Yoga, tantra, and bhakti, tellingly, arose, to greater and lesser degrees, as counter-cultural traditions, defining themselves in many ways against traditional elements of Hinduism, including doctrines of caste and an orthodox Brahmanical priestly hierarchy. Briefly tracing the history of these traditions can help clarify some of their differences and commonalities, though controversy and uncertainty persist. As my friend, Dr. Ravi Gupta, notes, "In this field of study, everything gets lost in pre-history."

Yoga and Renunciate Life

The *Upaniṣads* were said to have been composed (or received) by "forest dwellers"—renunciates who had left ordinary society to live ascetic lives in the forests and mountains, practicing meditation and seeking enlightenment. The word "yoga" ("union"), in the sense of spiritual practice, made its first appearance in world literature in one of these *Upaniṣads* —the *kaṭhopaniśad*—where it is defined as the stilling of the mind and senses to reach what is called "the unitive state." Yoga for some two thousand years continued as a meditative, spiritual practice to quiet the discursive mind and let the Divine Reality within come forth. Postural practice came much later and is a relatively new form of yoga (see below).

The tradition of renunciate forest dwellers living apart from conventional Vedic society was, even at the time, not a new phenomenon. Such a life is described in an ancient Vedic hymn, known as the "keśin hymn" (*Ṛgveda* 10.136). This hymn describes, with apparent admiration, the keśin, a "long-haired one," living outside ordinary Vedic society, wearing yellow rags or just the dust of the earth, spending time in contemplation, communing with the gods and flying through the air, being friend to both gods and mortals. "To look at him is like seeing heavenly brightness in its fullness. He is said to be light itself." (trans., Karel Werner). The keśin seems to be an early example of a yogi or (proto-)tantric practitioner, and like the forest-dwelling authors of the *Upaniṣads,* lived apart from society. The origins of this renunciate tradition are unknown and may have arisen from early indigenous tribal cultures or from the even more ancient Indus Valley Civilization of Northwest India (ca. 3500-1500), itself. The tradition continues today, and you can find these long-haired, celibate, wandering, mendicant yogis dressed in yellow, saffron, or orange meditating, chanting, and teaching at temples and sacred sites all over India.

Tantra

The esoteric tradition of tantra, or tantra yoga, is also of unknown and perhaps shamanistic origins. Textual evidence for the tradition, in the form of "tantras" or scriptures, began to appear in the early centuries of the first millennium CE. In Sanskrit, the suffix "tra," indicates an instrument ("mantra" being an instrument for "manas" the mind), and "tan," a verbal form meaning "to stretch or expand." Tantra is an instrument for expansion. It employs techniques including rituals, mantra recitation, visualization and meditation on cakras, mandalas, and deities, and a guru-disciple relationship to foster enlightenment and achieve union with the Divine. Many of the features we think of when we think of yoga today—cakras, nadīs, the subtle body, mandalas—come from tantra. (The Tibetan Buddhism of the Dalai Lama, as well, is a tantric form of Buddhism.)

The most important contribution tantra made to modern yoga, however, is the sacralization of the body. Earlier traditions of yoga tended toward asceticism, mastery, and transcendence of the body and the senses. Patañjali's *Yogasūtra* (400 CE), for example, the preeminent statement of classical yoga and the culmination of this approach, is based on *sāṃkhya* philosophy, a dualistic system that sees spirit and matter as eternally distinct. In this system, the problem we face is that our spirit (puruṣa) has become entangled in matter (prakṛti). The goal of yoga is the disentanglement—one might say the *dis-union*—of our spirit from matter and the body. Yoga (meditation) frees it. In the non-dualistic traditions of tantra, however, rather than seeing the body and matter as a problem or site of entanglement, both body and matter are considered manifestations or crystallizations of spirit. Spirit, even within form, is already free.

Because of this view of the body and the material world, tantra greatly facilitated the development of āsana and postural practice, using the body as a vehicle for liberation and union with the Divine, rather than seeing it as a site of entrapment. But Patañjali's classical yoga remained a meditative, not a bodily, practice, in which āsana simply meant "seat"—taking a seat for meditation. Yoga would have to wait another thousand before a text appeared which offered a series of non-seated āsanas and postures, the fifteenth century *Haṭhapradīpikā*, a text devoted to Lord Shiva.

Tantra remains a subject of fascination even today. Emphasizing the sacredness of all things, it has transgressive practices, including ritual sexual practices, designed to assist highly advanced practitioners in overcoming ingrained notions of conventional, dualistic thinking. In addition, tantra, perhaps because it may have derived from shamanism, has magical practices (though classical yoga, too, has practices for developing *siddhis*, or yogic powers.) Because of these features, two misconceptions about tantra persist: In India, tantra is often thought of as "black magic," and in the West, it is often thought of as "sexual yoga," both of which are inaccurate or misleading.

Bhakti

Bhakti is a path of yoga focused on love and devotion toward a personal form of the Divine. Beautiful passages of devotion to various gods can be found in the ancient hymns of the Vedas, but these hymns voice praise to largely inaccessible, awe-inspiring sky deities. In the latter half of the first millennium, BCE, however, two texts that would become central to Indian spirituality presented bhakti in terms of a personal relationship with Deity: The *Bhagavad Gītā* and the *Śvetāśvatara Upaniṣad.* In the *Gītā*, Krishna, a Divine avatar or incarnation of the god Viśnu, teaches the warrior Arjuna four kinds of yoga as paths to liberation. Bhakti yoga, Krishna says, the path of love, devotion, and surrender to the Divine, is the easiest and sweetest way to salvation. Similarly, the *Śvetāśvatara Upaniṣad* unfolds as a sublime, devotional text in worship of Lord Shiva, the Lord of Yoga.

Some centuries later, in the seventh-century, CE, in the southern state of Tamil Nadu, a powerful popular bhakti movement arose, which would spread throughout the subcontinent and remain central to the practice of Hinduism up to the present time. In communal chanting, singing, poetry, and dance, all dedicated to personal deities like Shiva or Krishna, new, passionate, even erotic, forms of bhakti found expression. Arising from within the lower classes and other groups traditionally excluded from the traditional Brahmanical religion, these burgeoning movements ignored entrenched systems of caste, class, and gender privilege. Salvific devotion to God was available to all, and all one needed was ecstatic love of one's *iṣṭadevattā* (cherished image for the Divine). In a developing collection of sacred texts known as the *Bhagavadpurāṇa*, stories of the love of Radha and the gopis (cowherds) for Lord Krishna offered scriptural authority for the practice of bhakti as the supreme path to salvation. Bhakti remains fundamental to Hindu religious practice today, and, once again, even though this tradition originally arose against many conventions of traditional Hinduism, Hinduism has absorbed and embraced it wholly.

Notes on the Meditations

अ *a* First letter.

Viṣnu is one of the high gods of what is often called the "Hindu Trinity," a trinity comprised of Brahmā, the creator, Viṣnu, the preserver, and Shiva, the destroyer or transformer. The universe in this system is eternal and moves through vast cycles of creation and destruction. In actual practice on the ground, however, we find more commonly the worship of the three gods, Viṣnu, Shiva, and Devī, the goddess, who herself manifests in numerous forms. Only a single temple to Brahmā exists in all of India. Contradiction and paradox are not a problem in Indian spirituality. Those who worship Rāma or Krishna or Shiva or Durgā, each see their own *iṣṭadevattā* (cherished form of the Divine) as ultimate and basically synonymous with the infinite Brahman. For example, worshippers of Shiva, the Lord of Yoga and Tantra, see Shiva as the creator, preserver, and destroyer. Followers of Krishna or Devī would see Krishna or Devī as fulfilling these same roles.

अ *a* अपरिग्रह *aparigraha* Non-attachment.

In Indian iconography, mythology, and theology, Lord Shiva most commonly appears in three forms. One is Shiva, the great meditator, who remains absorbed in meditation in his home, a cave on Mount Kailash in the Himālyas, sometimes for thousands of years. Second, is Shiva Naṭarāja, Lord of the Dance, pictured dancing the tāṇḍava, a whirling dance ringed in fire, the dance of the creation and destruction of the universe. Third, is Shiva the family man, featured with his partner, Pārvatī, and their two sons, Ganesha, the elephant headed god, and Kārtikeya, their philosopher-warrior son. There are other representations of Shiva, such as the terrifying form of Bhairava, who conquers demons, most particularly that of our ego.

ॠ *ṝ*

Many deities have terrifying forms, both in Shaiva and Shakta tantra as well as in traditions of Buddhism. These warrior forms of deities are said to destroy the obstacles to enlightenment, and ultimately, our ego, the limited, socially-constructed sense of a separate self, which stands in the way of our experience of our oneness with all reality.

ज *j*

In *samāsas*—compound nouns in Sanskrit—the first noun of the compound remains uninflected, undeclined, so the relationship between the two (or more) parts is ambiguous and fluid, determined largely by context. *Jyoti* is divine light, *prema* is divine love. The name can thus be translated as the joy of divine light, or the light of divine joy, the joy within light, the light within joy.

प *p*

In the *Ṛgveda*, the earliest scripture of India, an early hymn, No. 10.90, recounts a story of the creation of the universe. There are several creation stories in Hinduism and Indian spiritual systems, and in the Indian tradition, contradiction, as noted, is not seen as a problem. Here, the entire cosmos is envisioned as a single person, *Puruṣa*, and the sacrifice of this person by the gods provides the material for the formation of created things. The important thing to take away from this story is the centrality of sacrifice.

ह *h*

The scholar Finnian Gerety has shown that, in the Vedas, before the sacred syllable Oṃ appears, another sacred sound, *hiṃ*, seems to have been a precursor Oṃ. (*Ṛgveda* 1.164.26-28). *Hiṃ* is identified there as the sound of a mother cow calling her calves home to be fed. The mother cow is none other than a form of the goddess *vāc,* whose name means, speech, language, sound, and is the origin of all things.

Permissions

Thanks to these magazines for publishing the following meditations, sometimes in slightly different form:

“क, ka”	*Birmingham Poetry Review*
“उषस् *uṣas*”	*Braided Way*
“अग्नि, *agni,*”	*Five Points*
“ठ, ṭh,” “त, t,” “छ, ch,” “ऴ, lī”	*MuseIndia*
“र, r”	*Psaltery and Lyre*
“*ahāhata*” and “ai”	*Sufi Journal*
“ऐ, ai” and “ ग , ga”	*Sugar House Review*
ञ, ñ	*Bangalore Review*

About the Author

Longtime yoga and meditation teacher Michael David Sowder is an author, poet, and emeritus professor of poetry, religious studies, and yoga studies at Utah State University. With a PhD from the University of Michigan, Sowder is the author of two collections of spiritual poetry, *The Empty Boat* and *House Under the Moon*, and two chapbooks of poetry, including *A Calendar of Crows*. Feminist poet Diane Wakoski chose *The Empty Boat* to win the 2004 T.S. Eliot Award. *A Calendar of Crows*, won the inaugural New Michigan Press Poetry award.

Sowder's writing explores themes of yoga, Buddhism, mystical experience, contemplative practice, wilderness, and fatherhood. His work has appeared in *MuseIndia, The Bombay Review, Sufi Journal, Shambhala Sun* (now *Lion's Roar*), *American Life in Poetry, Five Points, Green Mountains Review, New Poets of the American West,* and *The New York Times Online*. He frequently travels to India, where in 2014, he was a Fulbright Scholar. Trained in a tantric yoga tradition, he has been practicing and teaching yoga and meditation for almost fifty years. The founder of the non-profit, Amrita Yoga Institute of Logan, Utah—which teaches yoga, meditation, contemplative practice and philosophy—he previously founded the first prison meditation program in the Alabama prison system in 1978 and has continued to teach in prisons and jails in the Intermountain West. He lives in Logan, Utah, at the foot of the Bear River Mountains with his partner, the writer Jennifer Sinor, and their children, Aidan Sowder-Sinor and Kellen Sowder-Sinor.

www.ingramcontent.com/pod-product-compliance
Lightning Source LLC
Jackson TN
JSHW020944250525
84197JS00001B/1